More Than a Carpenter

More Than
a Carpenter

JOSH McDOWELL
SEAN McDOWELL

TYNDALE
elevate
ask. seek. find.

Visit Tyndale online at tyndale.com.

Tyndale and Tyndale's quill logo are registered trademarks of Tyndale House Ministries. *Tyndale Elevate* and the Tyndale Elevate logo are trademarks of Tyndale House Ministries. Tyndale Elevate is a nonfiction imprint of Tyndale House Publishers, Carol Stream, Illinois.

More Than a Carpenter

Designed by Jennifer L. Phelps

The URLs in this book were verified prior to publication. The publisher is not responsible for content in the links, links that have expired, or websites that have changed ownership after that time.

For information about special discounts for bulk purchases, please contact Tyndale House Publishers at csresponse@tyndale.com, or call 1-855-277-9400.

Library of Congress Cataloging-in-Publication Data

A catalog record for this book is available from the Library of Congress.

ISBN 978-1-4964-8826-8

Printed in the United States of America

30	29	28	27	26	25	24
7	6	5	4	3	2	1

To Dick and Charlotte Day,
whose lives have always reflected that
Jesus was more than a carpenter

Contents

Preface

When I first sat down in 1976 with twelve legal pads, forty eight hours of free time, and a *lot* of coffee to write the book that would become *More Than a Carpenter*, I did so hoping it would help followers of Jesus to respond to questions about their faith and inspire spiritual seekers to honestly investigate the claims of Jesus. I never dreamed the story of my personal journey from skepticism to belief would ultimately sell more than seventeen million copies, be translated into over 120 languages, and inspire readers around the world to take a closer, deeper look at the possibility of faith. I continue to be honored and humbled each time someone tells me that my book made a difference in his or her life.

Yet I also continue to be struck by how much has happened in the world since *More Than a Carpenter* first released. Discoveries have been made (and continue to be made) that shed light on the historicity of Jesus Christ and the reliability of the Bible. New questions and challenges have emerged too. And while today's generation faces a whole host of new issues and choices, they also continue to confront the age-old questions: Who is Jesus? What proof is there that he was the Son of God? And even if it's true, what difference does it make to my life?

Based on all this, I decided it was time to give *More Than a Carpenter* another significant update. My son helped me with the last update (2009), so I invited him to join me again as a coauthor. Sean is a professor of apologetics at Talbot School of Theology, Biola University. He is a well-known speaker, writer, and YouTuber on various apologetics issues, including Jesus and the Bible. He has strong academic credentials (a double master's degree in philosophy and theology and a PhD in apologetics and worldview studies). The two of us worked together to revise existing material, add some new content, respond to popular objections, and give this classic book a fresh look. The result is a new edition of *More Than a Carpenter* that nonetheless retains its original hard-hitting examination of the facts and unapologetic search for truth. While Sean has substantially helped in updating this book, since it unfolds around my journey from skeptic to faith, we chose to keep it in my first-person voice.

It is our profound desire that this book will have a transformational impact on a new generation of people on a quest for spiritual clarity.

—JM

CHAPTER 1

My Story

Thirteenth-century philosopher Thomas Aquinas understood a deep truth: there is within every soul a thirst for happiness and meaning.[1] I first began to feel this thirst when I was a teenager. I wanted to be happy. I wanted my life to have meaning. I became hounded by those three basic questions that haunt every human life: What is my identity? What is my purpose? What is my destiny? I wanted answers, so as a young student, I started searching for them.

Where I was brought up, everyone seemed to be into religion, so I thought I might find my answers in being religious. I got into church 150 percent. I went every time the doors opened—morning, afternoon, or evening. But I must have picked the wrong church, because I felt worse inside it than I did outside. From my upbringing on a farm in Michigan I inherited a rural practicality that says when something doesn't work, get rid of it. So I chucked religion.

Then I thought education might have the answers to my quest for meaning, so I enrolled in a university. I soon became the most unpopular student among the professors. I would buttonhole them in their offices and badger them for answers to my questions. When they saw me coming, they would turn out the lights, pull down the shades, and lock their doors. You can learn many things at a university, but I didn't find the answers I was seeking. Faculty members and my fellow students had just as many problems, frustrations, and unanswered questions as I did.

One day on campus I saw a student wearing a T-shirt that read, "Don't follow me, I'm lost." That's how everyone in the university seemed to me. Education, I decided, was not the answer.

> **What do you think?**
>
> *Do you agree with Thomas Aquinas that every soul thirsts for happiness and meaning?*

I began to think maybe I could find happiness and meaning in prestige. I would find a noble cause, dedicate myself to it, and in the process, become well-known on campus. The people with the most prestige in the university were the student leaders, who also controlled the purse strings. So I got elected to various student offices. It was a heady experience to know everyone on campus, to make important decisions, to spend the university's money getting the speakers I wanted and the students' money for throwing parties.

But the thrill of prestige wore off like everything else I had tried. I would wake up on Monday morning, usually with a headache because of the night before, dreading to face another five miserable days. I endured Monday through Friday, living only for the partying nights of

Friday, Saturday, and Sunday. Then on Monday the meaningless cycle would begin all over again.

I didn't let on that my life was meaningless; I was too proud for that. Everyone thought I was the happiest man on campus. They never suspected that my happiness was a sham. It depended on my circumstances. If things were going great for me, I felt great. When things were going lousy, I felt lousy. I just didn't let it show.

> **Everyone thought I was the happiest man on campus. They never suspected that my happiness was a sham.**

I was like a boat out in the ocean, tossed back and forth by the waves. I had no rudder—no direction or control. But I couldn't find anyone living any other way. I couldn't find anyone who could tell me how to live differently. I was frustrated. No, it was worse than that. There's a strong term that describes the life I was living: *hell*.

About that time I noticed a small group of people—eight students and two faculty members—who seemed different from the others. They seemed to know who they were and where they were going. And they had convictions. It is refreshing to find people with convictions, and I like to be around them. I admire people who believe in something and take a stand for it, even if I don't agree with their beliefs.

It was clear to me that these people had something I didn't have. They were disgustingly happy. And their happiness

What do you think?
Do you like being around people with convictions? What makes it an invigorating experience? What makes it a frustrating one?

didn't ride up and down with the circumstances of university life; it was constant. They appeared to possess an inner source of joy, and I wondered where it came from.

Something else about these people caught my attention—their attitudes and actions toward each other. They genuinely loved each other—and not only each other but the people outside their group as well. And I don't mean they just talked about love; they got involved in people's lives, helping them with their needs and problems. It was totally foreign to me, yet I was strongly attracted to it.

Like most people, when I see something I want but don't have, I start trying to figure out a way to get it. So I decided to make friends with these intriguing people.

A couple of weeks later I sat around a table in the student union talking to some of the members of this group. The conversation turned to the topic of God. I was pretty skeptical and insecure about this subject, so I put on a big front. I leaned back in my chair, acting as if I couldn't care less.

"Christianity, ha!" I blustered. "That's for unthinking weaklings, not intellectuals." Of course, under all the bluster I really wanted what these people had, but my pride didn't want them to know the aching urgency of my need. The subject bothered me, but I couldn't let go of it. So I turned to one of the students, a good-looking woman (I used to think all Christians were ugly), and said, "Tell me, why are you so different from all the other students and faculty on this campus? What changed your life?"

Without hesitation, she looked me straight in the eyes, deadly serious, and uttered two words I never expected to hear in an intelligent discussion on a university campus: "Jesus Christ."

"Jesus Christ?" I snapped. "Oh, for God's sake, don't give me that garbage. I'm fed up with religion. I'm fed up with the church. I'm fed up with the Bible."

Immediately she shot back, "I didn't say *religion*, I said Jesus Christ!" She pointed out something I had never known: Christianity is uniquely about a relationship with God. Other religions focus on humans trying to work their way to God through good works. Christianity is God coming to us through Jesus Christ.

Other religions focus on humans trying to work their way to God through good works. Christianity is God coming to us through Jesus Christ.

I wasn't buying it. Not for a minute. Taken aback by the young woman's courage and conviction, I apologized for my attitude. "But I'm sick and tired of religion and religious people," I explained. "I don't want anything to do with them."

Then my new friends issued a challenge I couldn't believe. They challenged me to make a rigorous, intellectual examination of the claims of Jesus Christ—that he is God's Son; that he inhabited a human body and lived among real people; that he died on the cross for the sins of humanity; that he was buried and was resurrected three days later; and that he is still alive and can change a person's life even today.

I thought this challenge was a joke. Didn't everyone with any sense know that Christianity was based on a myth? I thought only a walking idiot could believe the myth that Christ came back from the dead. I used to wait for Christians to speak out in the classroom so I could tear them up one side and down the other. I thought that if a Christian had a brain cell, it would die of loneliness.

What do you think?
How would you define religion?

But I accepted my friends' challenge, mostly out of spite to prove them wrong. I was convinced the Christian story would not stand up to evidence. I was a prelaw student, and I knew something about evidence. I would investigate the claims of Christianity thoroughly and come back and knock the props out from under their sham religion.

I decided to start with the Bible. I knew that if I could uncover indisputable evidence that the Bible is not historically reliable, the whole of Christianity would crumble. Sure, Christians could show me that their own book said Christ was born of a virgin, performed miracles, and rose from the dead. But what good was that if the book was not a trustworthy account of these claims and events? If I could demonstrate *this*, then I could show that Christianity was a fantasy made up by wishful religious dreamers.

If I could uncover indisputable evidence that the Bible is not historically reliable, then I could show that Christianity was a fantasy made up by wishful religious dreamers.

I took the challenge seriously. I spent months in research. I even dropped out of school for a time to study in the historically rich libraries of Europe. To fund the trip, I sold a painting company I had started in college. And I found evidence. Evidence in abundance. Evidence I would not have believed had I not seen it with my own eyes. Finally I could come to only one conclusion: if I were to remain intellectually honest, I had to admit that the Old and New Testament documents were some of the most reliable writings in all of antiquity. And if they were reliable, what about this man Jesus, whom I had dismissed as a mere carpenter in an out-of-the-way town in a tiny, oppressed country, a man who had gotten caught up in his own visions of grandeur?

I had to admit that Jesus Christ was *more* than a carpenter. He was all he claimed to be.

> **I found evidence. Evidence in abundance. I had to admit that the Old and New Testament documents were some of the most reliable writings in all of antiquity.**

Not only did my research turn me around intellectually, but it also answered the three questions that started me on my quest for happiness and meaning. But hang in there, as I will tell you the rest of the story at the end of this book. First, I want to share with you the core of what I learned in my months of research so that you, too, may see that Christianity is not a myth, nor the fantasy of wishful dreamers, nor a hoax played on the simple-minded. It is rock-solid truth. And I guarantee that when you come to terms with that truth, you will be on the threshold of finding the answers to those three questions: What is my identity? What is my purpose? What is my destiny?

What do you think?

If God did become man, what would be the best way for him to communicate to his creation?

CHAPTER 2

What Makes Jesus So Different?

Sometime after my discoveries about the Bible and Christianity, I was riding in a cab in London and happened to mention something about Jesus to the driver. Immediately he retorted, "I don't like to discuss religion, especially Jesus." I couldn't help but notice the similarity of his reaction to my own when the young Christian woman told me that Jesus Christ had changed her life. The very name *Jesus* seems to bother people. It embarrasses them, angers them, or makes them want to change the subject. You can talk about God, and people don't necessarily get upset, but mention Jesus, and people want to stop the conversation. Why don't the names of the Buddha, Muhammad, or Confucius offend people the way the name of Jesus does?

I think the reason is that these other religious leaders didn't claim to be God. That is the big difference between Jesus and the others. It didn't take long for people who knew Jesus to realize that this carpenter from Nazareth was making

9

astounding claims about himself. It became clear that those claims were identifying him as more than just a prophet or teacher. He was obviously making claims to deity. He was presenting himself as the only avenue to salvation and the only source of forgiveness of sins—things they knew only God could claim.

> **What do you think?**
> Jesus said he was the Son of God. Why is that a problem for many people? Why is it less offensive to talk about God than Jesus?

For many people today Jesus' claim to be the unique Son of God is just too exclusive. In our pluralistic culture, it is too narrow and smacks of religious bigotry. We don't want to believe it. Yet the issue is not what we want to believe, but rather, who did Jesus claim to be? And is his claim true? That's what I desperately wanted to find out when I took up the challenge from my university friends.

I started by exploring all I could about the New Testament documents to see what they could tell us about this claim. I began to analyze the phrase "the deity of Christ" to see just what exactly was meant in the claim that Jesus Christ is God. Jews, Christians, and Muslims all agree that God is the perfect, eternal, all-knowing, and all-powerful creator of the universe. According to theists, God is a personal being who sustains the universe today. But Christian theism adds an additional note to the definition: God became incarnate as Jesus of Nazareth.

The name *Jesus* means "Jehovah-Savior" or "the Lord saves." The title *Christ* is derived from the Greek word for Messiah and means "anointed one."

The words *Jesus Christ* are not a first and last name; they are actually a name and a title. The name *Jesus* is derived from the Greek form of the name *Jeshua* or *Joshua*, meaning "Jehovah-Savior" or "the Lord saves." The title *Christ* is derived from the Greek word for Messiah (or the Hebrew *Mashiach*; see Daniel 9:26) and means "anointed one." The concept of Christ/Messiah in the Old Testament includes the offices of prophet, priest, and king. Before Jesus was born, Old Testament prophecies pointed to a coming deliverer who would fulfill all three roles. This affirmation is crucial to a proper understanding of Jesus and Christianity.

The New Testament clearly presents Jesus as God. Most of the names applied to Christ are such that they could properly be applied only to one who was God. For example, Jesus is called God in the statement "we look forward with hope to that wonderful day when the glory of our great God and Savior, Jesus Christ, will be revealed" (Titus 2:13; see also John 1:1; 20:28; Romans 9:5; Hebrews 1:8; 2 Peter 1:1; 1 John 5:20-21). The Scriptures attribute characteristics to him that can be true only of God. They present Jesus as being self-existent

The Scriptures attribute characteristics to Jesus that can be true only of God. Jesus received honor and worship that only God should receive.

(see John 1:2; 8:58; 17:5; 17:24), all-present (see Matthew 18:20; 28:20), all-knowing (see Matthew 17:22-27; John 4:16-18; 6:64), all-powerful (see Matthew 8:26-27; Luke 4:38-41; 7:14-15; 8:24-25; Revelation 1:8), and the source of eternal life (see 1 John 5:11-12, 20).

Jesus received honor and worship that only God should receive. In a confrontation with Satan, Jesus said, "The

Scriptures say, 'You must worship the LORD your God and serve only him'" (Matthew 4:10). Yet Jesus received worship as God from both humans and angels (see Matthew 14:33; 28:9, 17; John 5:23; Hebrews 1:6; Revelation 5:8-14). Most of the early followers of Jesus were devout Jews who believed in the one true God. They were monotheistic to the core, yet as the following examples show, they recognized him as God incarnate.

Because of the apostle Paul's extensive rabbinic training, he would be an unlikely person to attribute deity to Jesus, to worship a man from Nazareth and call him Lord. But this is exactly what Paul did. In his letter to the Colossians, Paul refers to Jesus as the "image of the invisible God" through whom "all things were created" and in whom "all the fullness of God was pleased to dwell" (Colossians 1:15, 16, 19, ESV).

After Jesus asked his disciples who they thought he was, Simon Peter confessed, "You are the Messiah, the Son of the living God" (Matthew 16:16). Jesus responded to Peter's confession, not by correcting his conclusion, but by acknowledging its validity and source: "You are blessed, Simon son of John, because my Father in heaven has revealed this to you. You did not learn this from any human being" (verse 17).

Martha, a close friend of Jesus, said to him, "I have always believed you are the Messiah, the Son of God" (John 11:27). Then there is the plainspoken Nathanael, who didn't believe anything good could come out of Nazareth. He admitted to Jesus, "Rabbi, you are the Son of God—the King of Israel!" (John 1:49). While the first Christian martyr, Stephen, was being stoned, he directed his dying prayer to Jesus: "Lord Jesus, receive my spirit" (Acts 7:59). The author of the book of Hebrews calls Christ God when he writes, "To the Son he says, 'Your throne, O God, endures forever and ever'" (Hebrews 1:8).

Then, of course, we have Thomas, better known as "the doubter." (Perhaps he was a graduate student.) He said, "I won't believe it unless I see the nail wounds in his hands, put my fingers into them, and place my hand into the wound in his side" (John 20:25). I identify with Thomas. He was saying, "Look, it's not every day that someone is raised from the dead or claims to be God incarnate. If you expect me to believe, I need evidence." Eight days later, after Thomas had expressed his doubts about Jesus to the other disciples, Jesus suddenly appeared. "'Peace be with you,' he said. Then he said to Thomas, 'Put your finger here, and look at my hands. Put your hand into the wound in my side. Don't be faithless any longer. Believe!' 'My Lord and my God!' Thomas exclaimed" (verses 26-28). Jesus accepted Thomas's acknowledgment of him as God. The apostle John and John the Baptist also refer to Jesus as God (see John 1:1, 14, 34). Those closest to Jesus consistently identified him as God in human flesh.

> **What do you think?**
> Would you consider yourself more of a Martha (always a believer) or a Thomas (a doubter) or a Nathanael (a cynic) in your attitudes about Jesus?

At this point a critic might interject that all these claims are from others about Christ, not from Christ about himself. People who lived at the time of Christ misunderstood him as we misunderstand him today. They attributed deity to him, but he didn't really claim it for himself.

Well, when we delve deeper into the pages of the New Testament, we find that Christ did indeed make this claim. Sometimes Jesus makes claims that clearly indicate his deity, but often those who heard him didn't understand. They frequently responded with questions such as, "Who does this man think he is?" While Jesus never uttered the exact words, "I am God," the weight of the New Testament is clear: Jesus claimed to be God. A businessman who scrutinized the Scriptures to verify whether Christ claimed to be God said to me, "Anyone who reads the New Testament and does not conclude that Jesus claimed to be divine would have to be as blind as a man standing outdoors on a clear day and saying he can't see the sun."

In the Gospel of John there is a confrontation between Jesus and a group of Jews. They criticize Jesus for claiming that Abraham anticipated his coming: "You are not yet fifty years old, and have you seen Abraham?" Jesus responds, "Truly, truly, I say to you, before Abraham was, I am" (John 8:57-58, ESV). As a result, they attempted to stone him. The phrase "I Am" is broadly understood to refer to the God of the Old Testament and was understood this way by Jesus' Jewish audience. (Their response indicates their instant recognition that such a statement made by a mere man would be blasphemy, deserving death.) For example, in the book of Exodus, God said to Moses, "I Am Who I Am. Say this to the people of Israel: I am has sent me to you" (Exodus 3:14). Interestingly, the Jewish audience questions him about his claims to have known the patriarch Abraham, but in response, he claims his own preexistence. Their response leaves little doubt that they understood his reference as a claim to be the God of the Old Testament. As a result of this interaction, and others in which Jesus makes his deity clear (e.g., John 5:17-18, 22-23), the religious leaders begin plotting to kill him. They not only hate him—they want him dead.

Jesus also made the radical claim to be one with the Father. You might say, "Look, Josh, I can't see how this proves anything. Didn't Jesus pray that he and the disciples and the Father would be one?" Yes, he did, but the context is different. During the Feast of Dedication in Jerusalem, some of the other Jewish leaders approached Jesus and questioned him about whether he was the Christ. Jesus concluded his comments to them by saying, "The Father and I are one" (John 10:30). "Once again the people picked up stones to kill him. Jesus said, 'At my Father's direction I have done many good works. For which one are you going to stone me?'" (verses 31-32). While it is true that Jesus prayed that he and the disciples and the Father would all be one in *unity* (see John 17:20-22), in John 10 Jesus claimed to be one in *nature* with God.

> **What do you think?**
>
> *Why do you think the Jewish leaders were so enraged with Jesus after he healed on the Sabbath? Was it because he did it on a sacred day or something else?*

One might wonder why the Jews reacted so strongly to what Jesus said about being one with the Father. The structure of the phrase in Greek gives us an answer. A. T. Robertson, the foremost Greek scholar of his day, writes that in Greek the word for *one* in this passage is neuter, not masculine, and does not indicate one in person or purpose but rather one in "essence or nature." Robertson adds, "This crisp statement is the climax of Christ's claims about the relation between the Father and himself (the Son). They stir the Pharisees to uncontrollable anger."[1] The Jewish leaders threatened Jesus with stoning for "blasphemy," which tells us that they definitely understood his claim to be God. But we may ask, did they stop to consider whether this claim was true?

What do you think?

The Jews wanted to stone Jesus for blasphemy. Was their own guilt over not believing him beginning to convict them? Or were they just jealous of his popularity?

Jesus consistently spoke of himself as one in essence and nature with God. He boldly asserted, "Whoever has seen me has seen the Father" (John 14:9, ESV). "Anyone who hates me also hates my Father" (John 15:23). "Everyone will honor the Son, just as they honor the Father. Anyone who does not honor the Son is certainly not honoring the Father who sent him" (John 5:23). These references indicate that Jesus looked at himself as being more than just a man; *he claimed to be equal with God*. Those who say that Jesus was just closer or more intimate with God than others need to consider his statement: "Anyone who does not honor the Son is certainly not honoring the Father who sent him."

While I was lecturing in a literature class at a university in West Virginia, a professor interrupted me and said that the only Gospel in which Jesus claimed to be God was John's Gospel, and it was the latest one written. He then asserted that Mark, the earliest Gospel, never once mentioned that Jesus claimed to be God.

This man simply had not read Mark carefully. In response

I turned to Mark's Gospel, to a passage in which Jesus claimed to be able to forgive sins. "Seeing their faith, Jesus said to the paralyzed man, 'My child, your sins are forgiven'" (Mark 2:5; see also Luke 7:48-50). According to Jewish theology, only God could say such a thing. Isaiah 43:25 restricts forgiveness of sin to the prerogative of God alone (see also Exodus 34:6-7; Psalm 51:4; Daniel 9:9). To the Jewish scribes steeped in the law of God, it was inconceivable that a man could forgive sins committed against God. When the scribes heard Jesus forgiving the man's sins, they asked, "What is he saying? This is blasphemy! Only God can forgive sins!" Jesus then asked which would be easier to say to a paralyzed man, "Your sins are forgiven" or "Stand up, pick up your mat, and walk" (Mark 2:7, 9).

According to *The Wycliffe Bible Commentary*, this is

> an unanswerable question. The statements are equally simple to pronounce; but to say either, with accompanying performance, requires divine power. An imposter, of course, in seeking to avoid detection, would find the former easier. Jesus proceeded to heal the illness that men might know that he had authority to deal with its cause.[2]

At this the religious leaders accused him of blasphemy. Lewis Sperry Chafer, founder and first president of Dallas Theological Seminary, writes,

Those who say that Jesus was just closer or more intimate with God than others need to consider his statement: "Anyone who does not honor the Son is certainly not honoring the Father who sent him."

None on earth has either authority or right to forgive sin. None could forgive sin save the One against whom all have sinned. When Christ forgave sin, as He certainly did, He was not exercising a human prerogative. . . . Since none but God can forgive sins, it is conclusively demonstrated that Christ, since He forgave sins, is God.[3]

This concept of forgiveness bothered me for quite a while because I didn't understand it. One day in a philosophy class, answering a question about the identity of Jesus, I quoted Mark 2:5. A graduate assistant challenged my conclusion that Christ's forgiveness of sin demonstrates his divine authority. He said that he could forgive people without the act demonstrating any claim to be God. People do it all the time.

What do you think?

In this instance, why do you think Jesus first said to the paralyzed man, "Your sins are forgiven" instead of "Stand up and walk"?

As I pondered what the man was saying, the answer suddenly struck me. I knew why the religious leaders reacted so strongly against Christ. Yes, someone can say, "I forgive you," but only if that person is the one who has been wronged. If you sin against me, I have the right to forgive you. But if you sin against someone else, I have no such right. The paralytic had not sinned against the man Jesus; the two men had never even seen each other before. *The paralytic had sinned against God.* Then along came Jesus, who under his own authority said, "Your sins are forgiven." Yes, we can forgive sins committed against us, but in no way can anyone forgive sins committed against

God except God himself. Yet that is what Jesus claimed to do. It's no wonder the Jews reacted so violently to the claims of Jesus! This assertion that he could forgive sin was a startling exercise of a prerogative that belongs only to God.

This is only one example from the Gospel of Mark. Let's briefly consider three more to show that it identifies Jesus as the Son of God. In 1:2-3, Mark cites a passage from Isaiah 40:3, which discusses how a messenger would come, like "the voice of one crying in the wilderness: 'Prepare the way of the Lord'" (ESV). This messenger would prepare the way "for our God." Mark substitutes Jesus as the Lord who is coming and John the Baptist as the messenger. In other words, John the Baptist is preparing the way for *God himself* to come in the person of Jesus Christ. The Gospel of Mark begins with the recognition that Jesus is the God of the Old Testament.

Mark also presents Jesus as *personally* claiming to be divine.

In Mark 6:45-52, Jesus walks on the water and his disciples are terrified to see him. He responds, "Take heart; it is I. Do not be afraid" (ESV). The Greek for "It is I" (*egō eimi*) is identical to how God revealed himself to Moses as "I Am" (Exodus 3:14). The linguistic similarity is not accidental.

We can forgive sins committed against us, but in no way can anyone forgive sins committed against God except God himself. Yet that is what Jesus claimed to do.

When Jesus says *egō eimi*, he is claiming to be the same divine figure who revealed himself to Moses in the burning bush. Thus, Jesus is making the same claim to deity here as recorded by John (see John 8:58).

Finally, the Gospel of Mark climaxes with Jesus claiming to be the Son of God at his trial. The high priest stands up and presses Jesus about his identity: "Are you the Messiah, the Son of the Blessed One?" Jesus responds, "I Am. And you will see the Son of Man seated in the place of power at God's right hand and coming on the clouds of heaven'" (Mark 14:61-62). Jesus' reference to "the Son of Man" who would be "coming on the clouds of heaven" was an allusion to Daniel 7:13-14 (NASB):

> I kept looking in the night visions,
> And behold, with the clouds of heaven
> One like a son of man was coming,
> And He came up to the Ancient of Days
> And was presented before Him.
> And to Him was given dominion,
> Honor, and a kingdom,
> So that all the peoples, nations, and populations
>   of all languages
> Might serve Him.
> His dominion is an everlasting dominion
> Which will not pass away;
> And His kingdom is one
> Which will not be destroyed.

While Jesus used the phrase "the Son of Man" through-out his ministry, it might have been unclear to his audience. But in this passage, at the climax of the Gospel of Mark,

Jesus reveals unmistakably what he meant all along. "Son of Man" is not a *lowly* title referring to his humanity but a *high* claim to be the majestic figure from heaven who is given glory, honor, and authority over all people and an eternal kingdom. In *Putting Jesus in His Place*, Robert Bowman and Ed Komoszewski explain how this applies to Daniel's vision:

> In Daniel's vision, the humanlike figure possesses all judgment authority and rules over an everlasting kingdom. The notion of frailty and dependence is absent. The description of the figure as coming with the clouds also identifies him as divine, since elsewhere in the Old Testament the imagery of coming on clouds is used exclusively for divine figures.[4]

Thus, in his allusion to Daniel 7:13, Jesus was claiming to be a divine, heavenly figure who would sit at God's right hand, exercising supreme authority over all people for eternity. No wonder the Jewish authorities were so upset—Jesus had committed blasphemy by claiming to be God! Clearly, Jesus believed he was divine in the Gospels of Mark *and* John.

An analysis of Christ's testimony shows that he claimed to be (1) the Son of the blessed God, (2) the one who would sit at the right hand of power, and (3) the Son of Man, who would come on the clouds of heaven. Each of these affirmations is distinctly messianic. The cumulative effect of all three is significant. The Sanhedrin, the Jewish court, caught all three points, and the high priest responded by tearing his garments and saying, "Why do we need other witnesses?" (Mark 14:63). They had finally heard it for themselves from Jesus' own mouth. He was convicted by his own words.

Sir Robert Anderson, who was once head of criminal investigation at Scotland Yard, points out,

> No confirmatory evidence is more convincing
> than that of hostile witnesses, and the fact that
> the Lord laid claim to Deity is incontestably
> established by the action of His enemies. We
> must remember that the Jews were . . . a highly
> cultured and intensely religious people; and
> it was upon this very charge that, without a
> dissentient voice, His death was decreed by
> the Sanhedrin—their great national Council,
> composed of the most eminent of their religious
> leaders, including men of the type of Gamaliel,
> the great first century Jewish philosopher and
> his famous pupil, Saul of Tarsus.[5]

It is clear, then, that this is the testimony Jesus wanted to bear about himself. We also see that the Jews understood his reply was a claim to be God. At this point they faced two alternatives: that his assertions were outlandish blasphemy or that he was God. His judges saw the issue clearly—so clearly, in fact, that they had him crucified and then taunted him because "he trusted God. . . . For he said, 'I am the Son of God'" (Matthew 27:43).

H. B. Swete, Regius professor of divinity at Cambridge University, explains the significance of the high priest tearing his garment:

The law forbade the High Priest to rend his garment in private troubles (Lev. X.6; xxi.10), but when acting as a judge, he was required by custom to express in this way his horror of any blasphemy uttered in his presence. . . . The relief of the embarrassed judge is manifest. If trustworthy evidence was not forthcoming, the necessity for it had now been superseded: the Prisoner had incriminated Himself.[6]

We begin to see that this was no ordinary trial. As lawyer Irwin Linton points out,

Unique among criminal trials is this one in which not the actions but the identity of the accused is the issue. The criminal charge laid against Christ, the confession or testimony or, rather, act in presence of the court, on which He was convicted, the interrogation by the Roman governor and the inscription and proclamation on His cross at the time of execution all are concerned with the one question of Christ's real identity and dignity. "What think ye of Christ? Whose son is he?"[7]

New York Supreme Court Justice William Jay Gaynor, in his address on the trial of Jesus, takes the position that blasphemy was the one charge made against him before the Sanhedrin. Referring to John 10:33, he says, "It is plain from each of the gospel narratives, that the alleged crime for which Jesus was tried and convicted was blasphemy.

In most trials the accused are tried for what they are alleged to have done, but this was not the case in the trial of Jesus. He was tried for *who he claimed to be*.

. . . Jesus had been claiming supernatural power, which in a human being was blasphemy."[8]

In most trials the accused are tried for what they are alleged to have done, but this was not the case in the trial of Jesus. He was tried for *who he claimed to be*.

The trial of Jesus should be sufficient to demonstrate convincingly that he confessed to his divinity. His judges attest to that claim. But also, on the day of Christ's crucifixion, his enemies acknowledged that he claimed to be God come in the flesh:

> The leading priests, the teachers of religious law, and the elders also mocked Jesus. "He saved others," they scoffed, "but he can't save himself! So he is the King of Israel, is he? Let him come down from the cross right now, and we will believe in him! He trusted God, so let God rescue him now if he wants him! For he said, 'I am the Son of God.'"
>
> MATTHEW 27:41-43

CHAPTER 3

Lord, Liar, or Lunatic?

Given the broad range of competing views about Jesus today, can we have confidence in the identity of the *real* Jesus? Many people want to regard Jesus not as God but as a good, moral man or as an exceptionally wise prophet who spoke many profound truths. Scholars often pass off that conclusion as the only acceptable one that people can reach by the intellectual process. Many people simply nod their heads in agreement and never trouble themselves to see the fallacy of such reasoning.

Jesus was not a legend but a historical figure who walked the earth roughly two thousand years ago. He claimed to be God, and to him it was of fundamental importance that men and women believed him to be who he was. We have already seen that Jesus' divine claims are attested in the earliest Gospel (Mark). Later in this book we will present evidence for the reliability of the Gospels. But for now, if we focus on his claims to be God, we have two choices: either we believe him, or we don't. He didn't leave us any wiggle room for in-between, watered-down alternatives.

C. S. Lewis, professor at Cambridge University and once an agnostic, understood this issue clearly. He writes,

> I am trying here to prevent anyone saying the really foolish thing that people often say about Him: "I'm ready to accept Jesus as a great moral teacher, but I don't accept His claim to be God." That is the one thing we must not say. A man who was merely a man and said the sort of things Jesus said would not be a great moral teacher. He would either be a lunatic—on a level with the man who says he is a poached egg—or else he would be the Devil of Hell. You must make your choice. Either this man was, and is, the Son of God: or else a madman or something worse.

Then Lewis adds, "You can shut Him up for a fool, you can spit at Him and kill Him as a demon, or you can fall at His feet and call Him Lord and God. But let us not come up with any patronizing nonsense about his being a great human teacher. He has not left that open to us. He did not intend to."[1]

"Let us not come up with any patronizing nonsense about [Jesus] being a great human teacher. He has not left that open to us. He did not intend to." —C. S. Lewis

Cambridge University professor F. J. A. Hort, who spent twenty-eight years in a critical study of the New Testament text, writes, "[Christ's] words were so completely parts and utterances of Himself, that they had no meaning as abstract statements of truth uttered by Him as a Divine oracle or prophet. Take away Himself as the primary (though not the ultimate) subject of every statement and they all fall to pieces."[2]

In the words of Kenneth Scott Latourette, historian of Christianity at Yale University, "It is not his teachings which make Jesus so remarkable, although these would be enough to give him distinction. It is a combination of the teachings with the man himself. The two cannot be separated." Latourette concludes,

> It must be obvious to any thoughtful reader of the Gospel records that Jesus regarded himself and his message as inseparable. He was a great teacher, but he was more. His teachings about the kingdom of God, about human conduct, and about God were important, but they could not be divorced from him without, from his standpoint, being vitiated.[3]

Jesus claimed to be God. His claim must be either true or false, and everyone should give it the same kind of consideration he expected of his disciples when he put the question to them: "Who do you say I am?" (Matthew 16:15). There are several alternatives.

First, consider that his claim to be God was false. If it was false, then we have only two alternatives. He either knew it was false, or he didn't know it was false. We will consider each possibility separately and examine the evidence for it.

Was Jesus a Liar?

If, when Jesus made his claims, he knew he was not God, then he was lying and deliberately deceiving his followers. But if he was a liar, then he was also a hypocrite because he modeled and taught the value of speaking the truth (see, for example, Matthew 5:37; John 8:44; 17:17; 18:37). Worse than that, if he was lying, he was evil because he told others to trust him for their eternal destiny as he deceived them with false hope. Last, he would also be a fool because his claims to being God led to his crucifixion—claims he could have backed away from to save himself even at the last minute.

> **What do you think?**
> Why can't we say that Jesus was just a good moral teacher? Can you think of any specific "good morals" that he taught his followers that still make sense today?

It amazes me to hear so many people say that Jesus was simply a good moral teacher. Let's be realistic. How could he be a great moral teacher and knowingly mislead people at the most important point of his teaching—his own identity?

To conclude that Jesus was a deliberate liar doesn't coincide with what we know either of him or of the results of his life and teachings. Wherever Jesus has been proclaimed, we see lives change for the good, nations change for the better, thieves become honest, alcoholics become sober, hateful individuals become channels of love, unjust persons embrace justice.

William Lecky, one of Great Britain's most noted historians and a fierce opponent of organized Christianity, saw the effect of true Christianity on the world. He writes,

It was reserved for Christianity to present to the
world an ideal which through all the changes
of eighteen centuries has inspired the hearts
of men with an impassioned love; has shown
itself capable of acting on all ages, nations,
temperaments, and conditions; has been not only
the highest pattern of virtue, but the strongest
incentive to its practice. . . . The simple record
of these three short years of active life has done
more to regenerate and soften mankind than
all the disquisitions of philosophers and all the
exhortations of moralists.[4]

Historian Philip Schaff says,

This testimony [that Jesus was God], if not true,
must be downright blasphemy or madness. . . .
Self-deception in a matter so momentous, and
with an intellect in all respects so clear and so
sound, is equally out of the question. How could
he be an enthusiast or a madman who never lost
the even balance of his mind, who sailed serenely
over all the troubles and persecutions, as the sun
above the clouds, who always returned the wisest
answer to tempting questions, who calmly and
deliberately predicted his death on the cross, his
resurrection on the third day, the outpouring of
the Holy Spirit, the founding of his Church, the
destruction of Jerusalem—predictions which have
been literally fulfilled? A character so original, so
complete, so uniformly consistent, so perfect, so
human and set so high above all human greatness,

can be neither a fraud nor a fiction. The poet, as
has been well said, would in this case be greater
than the hero. It would take more than a Jesus to
invent a Jesus.[5]

Elsewhere Schaff gives convincing argument against
Christ being a liar:

How in the name of logic, common sense, and
experience, could an imposter—that is a deceitful,
selfish, depraved man—have invented, and
consistently maintained from the beginning to
end, the purest and noblest character known in
history with the most perfect air of truth and
reality? How could he have conceived and carried
out a plan of unparalleled beneficence, moral
magnitude, and sublimity, and sacrificed his own
life for it, in the face of the strongest prejudices of
his people and age?[6]

Someone who lived as Jesus lived, taught as Jesus taught,
and died as Jesus died could not have been a liar. Let's look
at other alternatives.

Was Jesus a Lunatic?

If we find it inconceivable that Jesus was a liar, then couldn't
he have mistakenly thought himself to be God? After all, it's
possible to be both sincere and wrong. As we have seen in
chapter 2, Jesus didn't claim to be *a* god. He didn't claim to
be *a* divine being, or an angelic being. Through his words
and deeds, Jesus claimed to be *the* eternal, self-existent

creator of the universe. He said that whoever had seen him had seen God the Father (see John 14:9). He made himself equal to the one true God! For someone to mistakenly think himself God, especially in the context of a fiercely monotheistic culture, and then to tell others that their eternal destiny depended on believing in him, is no small pipe dream but delusional and self-centered. Can we honestly conclude that Jesus was likely delusional?

What do you think?

Why do you think Jesus took his message to the Jewish nation? Do you think there was any advantage to him being a carpenter before his ministry began?

Today we would treat someone who believed they were God the same way we would treat someone who believes he is Napoleon. We would see that person as deluded and self-deceived. Yet in Jesus we don't observe the characteristic imbalance that goes along with such delusions. If he really were delusional, his poise and composure were nothing short of amazing.

Harold Koenig, MD, is Professor of Psychiatry and Behavioral Sciences at Duke University Medical Center. He is the founding codirector of Duke's Center for Spirituality, Theology, and Health. He explains how unlikely it is that Jesus suffered from a delusional disorder:

> It is theoretically possible that someone could be suffering from a delusional disorder (believe he were God) and yet be highly functional in every other area of life. My experience when treating psychiatric patients, however, is that a person

with a delusional disorder has other symptoms that suggest that his/her thinking is not quite right. Given the profoundness of Jesus' teachings, the positive impact on mental health of Christian beliefs and practices, and the content of those teachings that emphasize the love of others and the care for others, even at cost to oneself, seem to me incompatible with the teachings of someone with a delusional disorder (where such delusions are usually self-centered, not other-centered). Jesus was anything but self-centered.[7]

In light of other things we know about Jesus, it's hard to imagine he suffered from a delusional disorder. Here is a man who spoke some of the most profound words ever recorded. His instructions have liberated many people from mental bondage. Practicing psychiatrist Pablo Martinez and Andrew Sims, former president of the Royal College of Psychiatrists, come to this conclusion about the mental state of Jesus:

> In summary, here we have someone with a coherent and profound message, an admired teacher; an individual with deep empathy and sympathy for the sick, the healer of the whole person; a man whose tender heart for the

What do you think?

Is there anything you detect in Jesus' behavior (other than his claim to divinity) that would suggest he was deluded? If you had lived in his day, would you have wanted to hear him?

oppressed and the marginalized aroused the
hostility of the establishment. Would anyone
dare to deny that this selfless and powerful
exercise of gifts reveals an exceptionally stable
character and an unsurpassable goodness?
No mentally sick person, no evil man, would
ever have been able to speak or behave in the
impeccable and influential way that Jesus
did. In our opinion, the evidence is again
convincing: Jesus was not only a man with
a balanced personality, but he also lived a
totally righteous life. If his character makes
him attractive, his words and deeds make him
unique. We find no discrepancy between his
being and his doing. The words and deeds of
Jesus plainly indicate extraordinary mental
health and unequivocal moral uprightness.[8]

Psychologist Gary R. Collins explains that

[Jesus] was loving but didn't let his compassion
immobilize him; he didn't have a bloated ego,
even though he was often surrounded by adoring
crowds; he maintained balance despite an often
demanding lifestyle; he always knew what he was
doing and where he was going; he cared deeply
about people, including women and children,
who weren't seen as important back then; he was
able to accept people while not merely winking
at their sin; he responded to individuals based
on where they were at and what they uniquely
needed. All in all, I just don't see signs that Jesus

was suffering from any known mental illness.
. . . He was much healthier than anyone else
I know—including me![9]

C. S. Lewis writes,

The historical difficulty of giving for the life,
sayings and influence of Jesus any explanation
that is not harder than the Christian explanation
is very great. The discrepancy between the depth
and sanity . . . of His moral teaching and the
rampant megalomania which must lie behind His
theological teaching unless He is indeed God has
never been satisfactorily explained. Hence the
non-Christian hypotheses
succeed one another with
the restless fertility of
bewilderment.[10]

What do you think?

Why do you think so
many mental health
professionals see Jesus
as a model for health?
Why was he so content?

Philip Schaff reasons, "Is
such an intellect—clear as the
sky, bracing as the mountain
air, sharp and penetrating as
a sword, thoroughly healthy and vigorous, always ready
and always self-possessed—liable to a radical and most serious delusion concerning his own character and mission?
Preposterous imagination!"[11]

Was Jesus Lord?

I cannot personally conclude that Jesus was a liar or a lunatic. The only other alternative is that he was—and is—the

34

Christ, the Son of God, as he claimed. But in spite of the logic and evidence, many people cannot seem to bring themselves to this conclusion.

When I discuss the material in this chapter with my Jewish and Muslim friends, their response is quite interesting. I share with them the claims Jesus made about himself and then put to them the options contained in the trilemma (liar, lunatic, or Lord?). When I ask if they believe Jesus was a liar, they give me a sharp "No!" Then I ask, "Do you believe he was a lunatic?" Their reply is "Of course not."

I cannot personally conclude that Jesus was a liar or a lunatic. The only other alternative is that he was—and is—the Christ, the Son of God, as he claimed.

"Do you believe he is God?" Before I can get a word in edgewise, I hear a resounding "Absolutely not!" Yet once we recognize that Jesus himself made this claim, we have no more choices.

The issue with these three alternatives is not which is logically possible, for obviously all three are possible. Rather, the question is "Which is most *probable*?" You cannot put him on the shelf merely as a great moral teacher or a prophet. That is not a valid option. He is either a liar, a lunatic, or Lord and God. You must make a choice. Your decision about Jesus must be more than an idle intellectual exercise. As the apostle John wrote in the climax of his Gospel, "These are written so that you may continue to believe that Jesus is the Messiah, the Son of God, and"—more important—"that by believing in him you will have life by the power of his name" (John 20:31).

The evidence is clearly in favor of Jesus as Lord.

CHAPTER 4

What about Science?

Many people resist personal commitment to Christ on the assumption that if you cannot prove something scientifically, it is therefore not true. Since one cannot scientifically prove the deity of Jesus or his resurrection, then modern sophisticates should know better than to accept him as Savior.

Often in a philosophy or history class someone confronts me with the challenge, "Can you prove it scientifically?" I usually say, "Well, no, I'm not a scientist." Then I hear the class chuckling and several voices saying things like "Then don't talk to me about it" or "See, you must take it all by faith" (meaning blind faith).

Once on a flight to Boston I was talking with the passenger next to me about why I personally believe Christ is who he claimed to be. The pilot, making his public relations rounds and greeting the passengers, overheard part of our conversation. "You have a problem with your belief," he said.

What do you think?

Besides historical facts, are there any other things we know to be true that are not provable scientifically? If so, what are they?

"What is that?" I asked.

"You can't prove it scientifically," he replied.

I am amazed at the inconsistency to which modern thinking has descended. This pilot is like so many people today who hold the opinion that if you can't prove a thing scientifically, it can't be known. But we all accept as true many facts that cannot be verified by scientific methods. We cannot scientifically prove anything about any person or event in history, but that doesn't mean history cannot be known. We need to understand the difference between the scientific method and what I call the legal-historical method. Let me explain.

The scientific method is based on drawing conclusions about the nature of something from replicable results that are consistent and clear. It is practiced in a controlled environment where observations can be made, data drawn, and hypotheses empirically verified. It is "related to measurement of phenomena and experimentation or repeated observation."[1] Dr. James B. Conant, former president of Harvard, writes, "Science is an interconnected series of concepts and conceptual schemes that have developed as a result of experimentation and observation, and are fruitful of further experimentation and observations."[2]

Many people today hold the opinion that if you can't prove a thing scientifically, it can't be known.

Testing the truth of a hypothesis by the use of controlled experiments is one of the key techniques of the modern scientific method. For example, someone claims that Ivory soap doesn't float. I claim it does. To prove my point, I take the doubter to the kitchen, put eight inches of lukewarm water in the sink, and drop in the soap. *Plunk!* We make observations, we draw data, and we verify my hypothesis empirically: Ivory soap floats.

If the scientific method were the only method we had for proving something, you couldn't prove that you watched a movie last night or that you had lunch today. There's no way we could repeat those events in a controlled situation. And we also couldn't prove that racism and sexism are wrong, since moral claims cannot be tested through the scientific method either. Whether through experience, testimony, or introspection, there are many things we can know outside the bounds of science.

Another method of investigation, the *legal-historical method*, is based on showing that something is a fact beyond a reasonable doubt. In other words, we reach a verdict on the weight of the evidence and have no rational basis for doubting the decision. Legal-historical proof depends on three kinds of testimony: oral testimony, written testimony, and exhibits (such as a gun, a bullet, or a notebook). Using the legal-historical method to determine the facts, you could prove beyond a reasonable doubt that you went to lunch today. Your friends saw you there, the waiter remembers seeing you, and you have the restaurant receipt.

If the scientific method were the only method we had for proving something, you couldn't prove that you had lunch today. There's no way we could repeat that event in a controlled situation.

Strictly speaking, the scientific method can be used to prove only repeatable things. Again, it isn't adequate for examining questions about persons or events in history. The scientific method isn't appropriate for answering such questions as Did George Washington live? Was Martin Luther King Jr. a civil rights leader? Who was Jesus of Nazareth? Was Jesus Christ raised from the dead? These questions belong in the realm of the legal-historical method. The scientific method is based on observation, information gathering, hypothesis, deduction, and experimental verification to find and explain empirical regularities in nature. As a result, it cannot uncover some of life's most important questions.

What do you think?

What are the advantages of using the scientific method to "prove" something? What are the disadvantages? What are the advantages of using the legal-historical method?

One thing about the Christian faith that has especially appealed to me is that it is not a blind, ignorant belief but rather one based on evidence. God did miracles through Moses so that the people would trust Moses as his spokesman and believe in him (see Exodus 14:31). Jesus did miracles largely to reveal his messianic identity so people could have a confident faith in his words and teachings (see Mark 2:10; John 20:30-31). Scripture doesn't call people to believe in *spite* of the evidence but in *light* of it. Every time we read that a Bible character was asked to exercise faith, we see that it's an intelligent faith. Jesus said, "You will know the truth" (John 8:32), not ignore it. Christ was asked, "Which is the most important commandment . . . ?" Jesus replied, "You must love the LORD your God with all your heart, all your soul, and *all your mind*" (Matthew 22:36-37, emphasis mine). Many people today seem to love God only with their hearts. The truth about Christ never gets to their minds. We've been given minds enabled by the Holy Spirit to know God, as well as hearts to love him and wills to choose him. We need to function in all three areas to have a full relationship with God and to glorify him. I don't know how it is with you, but my heart can't rejoice in what my mind has rejected. My heart and mind were created to work in harmony together. Never has anyone been called to check their brains at the door when trusting Christ as Savior and Lord. For me, it was the exact opposite.

In the next four chapters we will look at the evidence for the reliability of the written documents and for the credibility of the oral testimony and eyewitness accounts of Jesus.

CHAPTER 5

Is the New Testament Reliable?

The New Testament provides the primary historical source for information about Jesus. Because of this, in the past two centuries many critics have attacked the reliability of the biblical documents. There seems to be a constant barrage of charges that have no historical foundation or that have been proved invalid by archaeological discoveries and research.

While I was lecturing at Arizona State University, a professor who had brought his literature class approached me after an outdoor public lecture. He said, "Mr. McDowell, you are basing all your claims about Christ on a second-century document that is obsolete. I showed in class today that the New Testament was written so long after Christ lived that it could not be accurate in what it recorded." Essentially, he was arguing for late dating *and* that the New Testament documents are inaccurate. I think he is wrong on both counts!

I replied, "Sir, I understand your view, and I know the writings on which you base it. But the fact is, those writings have been proved wrong by more recently discovered documents that clearly show the New Testament to have been written within a generation of the time of Christ."

The source of that professor's opinions about the records concerning Jesus was the writings of the German critic Ferdinand Christian Baur. F. C. Baur assumed that most of the New Testament Scriptures were not written until late in the second century AD. How were they composed? He assumed the authors compiled myths and legends that had developed during the decades between the death of Jesus and the writing of the documents in the second century.

What do you think?

Have there been any biblical archaeological discoveries in recent years that grabbed your attention? Why do these discoveries often get world headlines?

Many theologically liberal scholars are being forced to consider earlier dates for the New Testament. The late Anglican bishop John A. T. Robinson's conclusions in his book *Redating the New Testament* are startlingly radical. His research led to his conviction that the whole of the New Testament was written before the fall of Jerusalem in AD 70.[1] While his assessment is earlier than most evangelical scholars would embrace, New Testament professor Jonathan Bernier has more recently made a solid case for an early dating of the New Testament. In his book *Rethinking the Dates of the New Testament*, Bernier concludes that "the majority of the texts that were eventually incorporated into the New Testament corpus were likely written twenty to thirty years earlier than is typically supposed by contemporary biblical scholars."[2] A good case can be made that all the New Testament books were written before the end of the first century.

Nonetheless, even if the Arizona professor was right about late dating, we would still have records of the events surrounding the origin of Christianity that are earlier than those sometimes used to support unquestioned events in history.

Sir William Ramsay, one of the greatest archaeologists ever to have lived, was a student at the German historical school, which taught that the book of Acts was a product of the mid-second century AD and not of the first century as it purports to be. After reading modern criticism about the book of Acts, Ramsay became convinced that it was not a trustworthy account of the facts of its time (AD 30–60) and therefore was unworthy of consideration by a historian. So in his research on the history of Asia Minor, Ramsay paid little attention to the New Testament. His investigation, however, eventually compelled him to reconsider the writings of Luke, the author of the book of Acts. The archaeologist observed the meticulous accuracy of the historical details, and gradually his attitude toward the book began to change. He was forced to conclude that "Luke is a historian of the first rank. . . . This author should be placed along with the very greatest of historians."[3]

Because of his belief in the book's accuracy, Ramsay finally conceded that Acts could not be a second-century document but belonged rather to the mid-first century. Since Ramsay's time, the case for the historical accuracy of Acts has developed considerably. In his four-volume commentary on Acts, leading New Testament scholar Craig

Keener goes to great lengths to assess the historicity of Acts in terms of ancient historiography. He notes that there is frequent external corroboration for people, places, and events in Acts and that eyewitness testimony lies behind it. Dr. Keener concludes, "As historical sources go, Acts is an extremely valuable one, offering serious evidence of dependence on considerable eyewitness testimony."[4]

Today, the form critics—scholars who analyze the ancient literary forms and oral traditions behind the biblical writings—say that the material was passed by word of mouth until it was written down in the form of the Gospels. Even though they now admit the period of transmission to be much shorter than previously believed, they still conclude that the Gospel accounts took on the forms of folk literature (legends, tales, myths, and parables).

However, one of the major charges against the form critics' concept of oral tradition development is the short length of time between the New Testament events and the recording of them. Speaking of the brevity of this interval, Simon Kistemaker, professor of New Testament at Reformed Theological Seminary, writes,

> Normally, the accumulation of folklore . . . takes many generations; it is a gradual process spread over centuries of time. But in conformity with the thinking of the form critic, we must conclude that the Gospel stories were produced and collected within little more than one generation. In terms of the form-critical approach, the formation of the individual Gospel units must be understood as a telescoped project with accelerated course of action.[5]

A. H. McNeile, Regius Professor of Divinity at the University of Dublin, challenges form criticism's concept of oral tradition. He points out that form critics do not deal with the tradition of Jesus' words as closely as they should. In the Jewish culture it was important that a teacher's words were carefully preserved and passed down.[6] It was customary for a Jewish student to memorize a rabbi's teaching and pass it on with utmost care. For example, in 1 Corinthians 7:10, 12, Paul shows this concern for both preserving the teachings of Jesus and distinguishing them from his own: "To the married I give this charge (not I, but the Lord): the wife should not separate from her husband. . . . To the rest I say (I, not the Lord) . . ." (ESV).

In the Jewish culture it was important that a teacher's words were carefully preserved and passed down.

Other scholars concur. Paul L. Maier, a professor of ancient history at Western Michigan University, writes, "Arguments that Christianity hatched its Easter myth over a lengthy period of time or that the sources were written many years after the event are simply not factual."[7] The New Testament remains firmly grounded in history.

Four Gospels or More?

Whether in books, movies, or even sometimes in the scholarly world, the claim is often made that, while Matthew, Mark, Luke, and John were selected to be part of the New Testament, several other "gospels" were also in the running to be included. The most notable examples are those of Thomas, Judas, Philip, Peter, and Mary. The implication is clear: these ancient texts reveal a different view of Jesus that is just as valid as the time-honored tradition of the church.

Is there any truth to these claims? Have the four Gospels lost their privileged status as unique purveyors of the life and ministry of Jesus? Are these recently uncovered gospels transforming our understanding of Christianity?

What do you think?

Do you give any credence to books, articles, or TV documentaries with extrabiblical information about the credibility and historicity of Jesus? How would you compare the historical evidence for Jesus with that for other well-known persons?

As extraordinary and dramatic as such claims may seem, they simply fall apart under the weight of historical analysis. In *Hidden Gospels*, historian Philip Jenkins concludes that the "idea that the various noncanonical gospels are equally valid witnesses to Christian antiquity is deeply flawed."[8] The most serious challenge to the status of these other gospels is their late dating. While the four Gospels were all written within the first century, all evidence points to these other gospels being composed between AD 120 and 250, at least two to three generations removed from the life of Christ.

Because these texts are written so much later than the four traditional Gospels, it is unlikely that they reveal any novel information about the historical Jesus. Thus, New Testament professor Craig A. Evans concludes, "The scholarly track record with respect to the use of these extracanonical Gospels is, frankly, embarrassing. . . . We

48

have found that these extracanonical Gospels do not offer early, reliable tradition, independent of what we possess in the New Testament Gospels."[9]

Evidence for the New Testament

Often non-Christians tell me that we can't trust what the Bible says. "Why, it was written more than two thousand years ago. It's full of errors and discrepancies," they say. I reply that I believe I can trust the Scriptures. Then I describe an incident that took place during a lecture in a history class. I stated that I believed there was more evidence for the reliability of the New Testament than for almost any other ten pieces of classical literature put together.

The professor sat in the corner snickering, as if to say, "Oh, come on now, you can't believe that." I asked him what he was laughing about. He replied, "I can't believe you have the audacity to claim in a history class that the New Testament is reliable. That's ridiculous!"

Wanting to find common ground for discussion, I asked him, "Tell me, sir, as a historian, what are the tests that you apply to any piece of historical writing to determine its accuracy and reliability?" I was amazed that he did not have any such tests. It is astonishing how few people can answer this question. "I have some tests," I answered. I told him that I strongly believe we should test the historical reliability of the Scriptures by the same rigorous criteria that we apply to other historical documents. Military historian Chauncey Sanders lists and explains the three basic principles of historiography: the *bibliographical* test, the *internal evidence* test, and the *external evidence* test.[10] Let's examine each one.

Bibliographical Test

The bibliographical test checks how accurately an ancient document has been copied and passed down across history. This test is necessary because we do not have the original manuscripts of the Bible (the *autographs*). Instead, we have handwritten copies of copies of copies of the Bible called *manuscripts*. Each manuscript is slightly different because of intentional or unintentional changes. So, by utilizing the bibliographical test, we ask, Can we confidently piece together the original text of the Bible using the manuscripts that exist today? Typically this conversation centers around the New Testament in particular, so we will focus our inquiry there.

In order to recreate the original text of the Bible, it helps to have a large number of manuscripts to work with so that we can compare them against each other. Three different manuscripts may not be very helpful, but three hundred different manuscripts will reveal patterns, trends, and similarities to give us a better chance of reconstructing the original text. This is good news for the Christian, because of all the ancient writings we have, the New Testament far outshines the others in terms of manuscript quantity. Most ancient writings have (maybe) a couple hundred manuscripts to their name, which is sufficient. Comparatively, at the time of this writing, the Institute for New Testament Textual Research (INTF) lists the number of manuscripts to the New Testament at 5,700.[11] The next runner-up is Homer's *Iliad*, which boasts around 1,900 manuscripts.[12]

However, manuscripts are not merely counted. They are also weighed. In most cases, earlier manuscripts are given more weight of consideration because a smaller time gap between a manuscript and the original text would likely mean that there are fewer copies in between. The problem is that earlier manuscripts also tend to be small fragments of what they originally were, providing only a verse or a couple of words of the Bible. So, the question remains: Do we have enough useful data *across our earliest manuscripts* to recreate the original text?

What do you think?

Do you or someone you know believe that because the Bible text is ancient, it can't be trusted? Are there other nonbiblical ancient texts that you or they have no problem trusting?

Yes! Daniel Wallace, professor of New Testament studies at Dallas Theological Seminary and one of the world's leading authorities on the Greek text and New Testament manuscripts, states, "Today we have as many as 12 MSS [i.e., manuscripts] from the second century, 64 from the third, and 48 from the fourth—a total of 124 MSS within 300 years of the composition of the NT [i.e., New Testament]. Most of these are fragmentary, but the whole NT text is found in this collection multiple times."[13]

Think about it: given that a typical manuscript could last over a century (and some scholars estimate even longer), the earliest manuscripts we have today may be only a couple of generations removed from the original. This would cause some differences across the manuscripts due to human error, but we would not expect the differences to be so substantial that the original text cannot be recovered with a high degree of confidence. Even some of our older, more complete medieval manuscripts give evidence that they were copied from very early manuscripts which we no

When it comes to the manuscript authority of the New Testament, the abundance of material is truly remarkable. We can have great confidence that an authentic New Testament text has been established.

longer have, effectively giving them a comparable status with our earliest ones.[14]

When it comes to the manuscript authority of the New Testament, the abundance of material is truly remarkable. If we add to that authority the more than 140 years of intensive work evaluating New Testament manuscripts with our modern techniques, we can have great confidence that an authentic New Testament text has been established. Italian classical scholar Giorgio Pasquali concludes about the New Testament, "No other Greek text is handed down so richly and credibly."[15]

Some may still object and say that the text of our Bible could have been changed dramatically before our earliest manuscripts. This is certainly *possible*, but is it *reasonable*? The bulk of manuscripts, spanning over a thousand years, show relatively little change. Why should we think the manuscripts were hopelessly corrupted within the first one or two hundred years? Even if someone wanted to intentionally change the contents of the Bible, no one could travel the Middle Eastern world to find and change all the manuscripts without the churches noticing. For this to work, they would have had to access the text of the Gospels before they were copied and spread around the world. But how would they have known that the text was important enough to mess with until after it was already spreading? The theory of a corrupted text prior to our earliest manuscripts cannot hold water.

What about Biblical Variants?

Textual critic Bart Ehrman created a firestorm of controversy with the release of his bestselling book *Misquoting Jesus*. His claim was simple: the New Testament manuscripts have so many errors that they undermine an evangelical view of the inspiration of Scripture. He does believe it is meaningful to talk about the original text and that we should try to recover it. But he emphasizes the significance of the variants. Some of these mistakes were accidental, claims Ehrman, while others were intentional. This raises a vital question: Can we trust the New Testament amid the manuscript variants?

Ehrman claims there are 300,000 to 400,000 variants among New Testament manuscripts. Simply put, a textual variant is any time the New Testament manuscripts have alternative wordings. Given that the Greek New Testament of today has roughly 138,000 words, the idea that there are two to three times as many variants as words is unsettling. (Truth be told, the number of non-spelling variants is probably closer to 500,000 in Greek manuscripts alone.[16])

Yet the large number of variants is a direct result of the extremely large number of New Testament manuscripts that we have. In other words, we have so many variants because we have such a plethora of manuscripts! In his PhD thesis at the University of Birmingham, Michael Morrill collected all the variants in John 18 and recorded 3,058 unique variants for that chapter, or about 3.9 variants per word.[17] Although this may seem devastating, New Testament professor Peter Gurry points out that this means the average manuscript has about one variant every 434 words. For a scribe copying by hand in candlelight, that's not bad![18] Maybe a letter was copied twice or a word was skipped over. But when we compare the various manuscripts and the different kinds of variants, we can reconstruct John 18 (and the rest of the New Testament) with a high degree of confidence.

Do not misunderstand me: there are some challenges in the New Testament text that are both significant and difficult to deal with. But those are *exceptions*. When all variations are considered, roughly one percent involve the meaning of the text. But even this fact can be overstated. For instance, there is disagreement about whether 1 John 1:4 should be translated, "We are writing these things so that *our* joy may be complete" or "We are writing these things so that *your* joy may be complete." While this disagreement does involve the meaning of the passage, it in no way jeopardizes a central doctrine of the Christian faith. This is why the authors of *Reinventing Jesus* conclude, "The short answer to the question of what theological truths are at stake in these variants is—none."[19] After all, even when an important biblical passage has difficult textual variants, Christian theology does not hang on any single verse. It is upheld by a web of data from all across Scripture.

Internal Evidence Test

The bibliographical test determines only that the text we have now is what was originally recorded. One has still to determine not only whether that original written record is credible but also to what extent it is credible. That is the task of internal criticism, which is the second test of historicity cited by Chauncey Sanders.

Apologist John W. Montgomery reminds us that "historical and literary scholarship continues to follow

Aristotle's eminently just dictum that the benefit of doubt is to be given to the document itself, not arrogated by the critic to himself." Montgomery continues, "This means that one must listen to the claims of the document under analysis, and not assume fraud or error unless the author disqualifies himself by contradictions or known factual inaccuracies."[20]

Louis Gottschalk, professor of history at the University of Chicago, outlines his historical method in a guide used by many for historical investigation. Gottschalk points out that the ability of the writer or the witness to tell the truth is helpful to historians in their effort to determine credibility, "even if it is contained in a document obtained by force or fraud, or is otherwise impeachable, or is based on hearsay evidence, or is from an interested witness."[21]

This ability to tell the truth is closely related to the witness's nearness both geographically and temporally to the events recorded. The New Testament accounts of the life and teaching of Jesus were recorded by men who had either been eyewitnesses themselves or who carefully related the accounts of eyewitnesses of the actual events or teachings of Christ. Consider the opening to Luke's Gospel:

> Many people have set out to write accounts
> about the events that have been fulfilled among
> us. They used the eyewitness reports circulating
> among us from the early disciples. Having carefully
> investigated everything from the beginning, I also
> have decided to write a careful account for you,
> most honorable Theophilus, so you can be certain
> of the truth of everything you were taught.
>
> LUKE 1:1-4

Luke was not an eyewitness of the events he records, but he begins his Gospel with this short preface so that readers will know his concern for truth. Luke is signaling to his readers that he has carefully investigated the events he records and is not reporting hearsay. Luke is not the only biblical writer concerned with accurate reporting. Consider some other accounts:

> We were not making up clever stories when we told you about the powerful coming of our Lord Jesus Christ. We saw his majestic splendor with our own eyes.
>
> 2 PETER 1:16

> We proclaim to you what we ourselves have actually seen and heard so that you may have fellowship with us. And our fellowship is with the Father and with his Son, Jesus Christ.
>
> 1 JOHN 1:3

> This report is from an eyewitness giving an accurate account. He speaks the truth so that you also may continue to believe.
>
> JOHN 19:35

> During the forty days after he suffered and died, he appeared to the apostles from time to time, and he proved to them in many ways that he was actually alive. And he talked to them about the Kingdom of God.
>
> ACTS 1:3

Peter and John replied, . . . "We cannot stop telling about everything we have seen and heard."

ACTS 4:19-20

As we have seen, the New Testament books consistently claim to be written by witnesses, but how do we know we can trust these claims? J. Warner Wallace is a cold case detective who was an atheist until he was thirty-five. He is frequently interviewed on television crime series because of his success as a detective. He previously assumed the biblical narrative was mythological until he read through the book of Acts. Wallace was struck by how the apostles repeatedly call upon their eyewitness testimony as the basis for their preaching and teaching. He decided to apply the rules of forensic science to the Gospels. He came to four key conclusions. First, the Gospel writers were present at the events they recorded. According to Wallace, "Their testimony appears early enough in history to confirm they were actually present to see what they said they saw."[22]

What do you think?

After reading these biblical eyewitness accounts, what words or phrases do they use that make you carefully consider their claims? What emotion seems to reverberate in these accounts?

Using forensic analysis, he also concludes that they were accurate and honest in their testimony over time, that their testimonies can be verified, and that there is no convincing ulterior motive to account for their proclamation of a crucified savior. Not only was detective Wallace convinced the Gospel writers were eyewitnesses, but he also later became a follower of Jesus.

There is an additional point that helps establish the trustworthiness of the apostles' testimony: *the New Testament accounts of Christ were being circulated within the lifetimes of his contemporaries.* Why does this matter? These people whose lives overlapped with Jesus and the proclamations of the Gospel writers could certainly confirm or deny the accuracy of the accounts. In advocating their case for the gospel, the apostles had appealed (even when confronting their most severe opponents) to common knowledge concerning Jesus. They not only said, "Look, we saw this" or "We heard that," but they turned the tables and said right in the face of adverse critics, "You also know about these things. You saw them. You yourselves know about it." Listen to the challenge in the following passages:

> Men of Israel, listen to these words: Jesus the Nazarene, a Man attested to you by God with miracles and wonders and signs which God performed through Him in your midst, just as *you yourselves know.*
>
> ACTS 2:22, NASB, *emphasis added*

Suddenly, Festus shouted, "Paul, you are insane.
Too much study has made you crazy!"

But Paul replied, "I am not insane, Most
Excellent Festus. What I am saying is the sober
truth. And *King Agrippa knows about these things.*
I speak boldly, for I am sure these events are
all familiar to him, for they were not done in a
corner!"

ACTS 26:24-26, *emphasis added*

One had better be careful when telling the opposition,
"You know this also," because if there isn't common knowledge and agreement of the details, the challenge will be
shoved right back.

Concerning this primary-source value of the New
Testament records, F. F. Bruce observes,

It was not only friendly eyewitnesses that
the early preachers had to reckon with; there
were others less well-disposed who were also
conversant with the main facts of the ministry
and death of Jesus. The disciples could not
afford to risk inaccuracies (not to speak of
willful manipulation of the facts), which would
at once be exposed by those who would be only
too glad to do so. On the contrary, one of the
strong points in the original apostolic preaching
is the confident appeal to the knowledge of the
hearers; they not only said, "We are witnesses of
these things," but also, "As you yourselves also
know" (Acts 2:22). Had there been any tendency
to depart from the facts in any material respect,

the possible presence of hostile witnesses in
the audience would have served as a further
corrective.[23]

The events surrounding Jesus were not done in private.
He taught in public. He performed miracles in public. He
was crucified in public. And he was buried in a known
man's tomb. If the claims about the life and events regard-
ing Jesus were not true, hostile witnesses would have been
quick to correct the record. And yet the apostles proclaimed
their message in the presence of such enemies. Minimally,
this shows remarkable confidence in the correctness of their
beliefs about Jesus.

This is one reason renowned educator and historian
David Hackett Fischer considered the eyewitness testimony
of the apostles to be "the best relevant evidence."[24]

Historian Will Durant was trained in the discipline of
historical investigation and spent his life analyzing records
of antiquity. He did not take a conservative view of the
Gospels, yet because of his careful historical approach, he
was forced to concede that much of the Gospels reported
historical fact. Durant writes,

> Despite the prejudices and theological
> preconceptions of the evangelists, they record
> many incidents that mere inventors would have
> concealed—the competition of the apostles for
> high places in the Kingdom, their flight after
> Jesus' arrest, Peter's denial, the failure of Christ
> to work miracles in Galilee, the references of
> some auditors to his possible insanity, his early
> uncertainty as to his mission, his confessions

of ignorance as to the future, his moments of bitterness, his despairing cry on the cross; no one reading these scenes can doubt the reality of the figure behind them. That a few simple men should in one generation have invented so powerful and appealing a personality, so lofty an ethic and so inspiring a vision of human brotherhood, would be a miracle far more incredible than any recorded in the Gospels. After two centuries of Higher Criticism the outlines of the life, character, and teaching of Christ, remain reasonably clear, and constitute the most fascinating feature in the history of Western man.[25]

External Evidence Test

The third test of historicity is that of external evidence. The issue here is whether other historical material confirms or denies the internal testimony of the documents themselves. In other words, what sources, apart from the literature under analysis, substantiate the document's accuracy, reliability, and authenticity?

One way to externally corroborate the New Testament is through other ancient writings. As perhaps the world's leading expert on the historical resurrection of Jesus, Gary Habermas has extensively studied the extrabiblical evidence

> **The third test of historicity is that of external evidence— whether other historical material confirms or denies the internal testimony of the documents themselves.**

for Jesus. "When the combined evidence from ancient non-Christian sources is summarized," says Habermas, "quite an impressive amount of information is reported concerning Jesus and ancient Christianity." This information includes that Jesus (1) lived and ministered in Palestine, (2) was reportedly born of a virgin, (3) had a brother named James, (4) came from a poor family, (5) was known as a wise and virtuous man, (6) had both Jewish and Gentile disciples, (7) was worshiped as deity, (8) performed miracles, (9) offered prophecies that were fulfilled, (10) cast out demons, (11) was crucified under Pontius Pilate, and much more.[26] Given that Jesus lived in an obscure part of the Roman Empire, had no military or government post, and had a public ministry that lasted just two to three years, it is surprising how much information we *do* have about him from extrabiblical sources. And we have much more when we consider other parts of the New Testament, such as the life and travels of Paul.

What do you think?

Even with archaeological evidence, critics often state that the Scriptures are not historically accurate. Why do you think that's the case? Is there any evidence that would be irrefutable for you?

Archaeology also provides powerful external evidence. It contributes to biblical criticism, not in the area of inspiration and revelation, but by providing evidence of accuracy concerning the events recorded. Many scholars and media sources consider the Bible to be myth, legend, or propaganda. It is often dismissed as irrelevant for historical study. "And yet," writes archaeologist Titus Kennedy, "when people look into what archaeologists have unearthed, a different story comes to light, showing that instead of fiction and fairy tales, archaeology indicates that the Bible preserves an accurate recounting of the history addressed in its pages. Specifically, hundreds of artifacts from the distant past have demonstrated the events, people, and places in the Bible to be historical."[27] In his book *Unearthing the Bible*, Dr. Kennedy lists 101 archaeological discoveries—from Genesis to the book of Acts—that illuminate and confirm the Bible.

We have already seen how archaeology led Sir William Ramsay to change his initial negative convictions about the historicity of Luke. As a result, he concluded that the book of Acts was accurate in its description of the geography, antiquities, and society of Asia Minor.

F. F. Bruce notes that "where Luke has been suspected of inaccuracy, and accuracy has been vindicated by some inscriptional [external] evidence, it may be legitimate to say that archaeology has confirmed the New Testament record."[28]

"But Josh," you might be wondering, "aren't fictional stories also told in realistic settings? If the New Testament writers wanted to pawn off their story as true, it would make sense to give it a realistic backdrop." This is a fair response. But for two reasons I am not convinced. First, the biblical writers didn't have modern digital technology to research people, places, and events. Yet it turns out that the evangelists knew a lot about the geography, locations where Jesus ministered, customs, and culture of the day. As Lydia McGrew demonstrates in her book *Testimonies to the Truth: Why You Can Trust the Gospels*, this points to the apostles being genuine witnesses to the events they report.[29]

Second, remember that the New Testament writers frequently claim to be reporting truth. Rather than passing on myths, the New Testament writers present the apostles as witnesses (see 2 Peter 1:16). Since the New Testament writers claim to care about the facts, an investigation of the facts would be helpful. Thus, the external test can help us examine if their internal claims are true. In the case of the New Testament, the external case is powerful.

If we discard the Bible as unreliable historically, then we must discard all the literature of antiquity.

After personally trying to shatter the historicity and validity of the Scriptures, I have been forced to conclude that they are historically trustworthy. If we discard the Bible as unreliable historically, then we must discard all the literature of antiquity. No other ancient book has as much evidence to confirm its reliability. One problem I encounter constantly is the tendency to apply one standard to test secular literature and another to the Bible. We must apply the same standard, whether the literature under investigation is secular or religious. Having done this myself, I am convinced that the Bible is trustworthy and historically reliable in its witness about Jesus.

CHAPTER 6

Who Would Die
for a Lie?

Those who challenge Christianity often overlook one area of evidence: the transformation of Jesus' apostles. The radically changed lives of these men give us solid reason to trust their testimonies about Christ.

Since the Christian faith is historical, our knowledge of it must rely heavily on testimony, both written and oral. Without such testimony, we have no window to any historical event, Christian or otherwise. In fact, all history is essentially a knowledge of the past based on testimony. If reliance on such testimony seems to give history too shaky a foundation, we must ask, How else can we learn of the past? How can we know that Napoleon lived? None of us was alive in his time period. We didn't see him or meet him. We must rely on testimony.

Thus, our knowledge of history has one inherent problem: Can we trust that the testimony is reliable? Since our knowledge of Christianity is based on testimony given in the distant past, we must ask whether we trust those who wrote it. Do we have reason to believe they have the character and ability to correctly convey what Jesus said and did? I believe we can.

One reason I trust the apostles' testimonies is because the apostles were willing to suffer and die for their belief that Jesus had risen from the dead. These men willingly put themselves in harm's way, which involved getting mocked, thrown in prison, beaten, and even killed for their faith. Just read the first few chapters in Acts!

My son Sean did his PhD dissertation on the fate of the apostles and has published an academic analysis of the evidence. What did he find? First, the apostles were willing to suffer for their belief that Jesus had risen. The earliest accounts we have of what the first Christians believed, such as the short summary of Christian belief in 1 Corinthians 15:3-5, are consistently tied to belief in the Resurrection. Second, there was persecution against the early church—first from the religious leaders and then later from Rome. Third, we have solid historical evidence that at least some of the twelve disciples died as martyrs, as well as the apostle Paul and James, the brother of Jesus. Fourth, there is no evidence any of them recanted.

It is important to keep in mind that the willingness of the apostles to suffer and die for their faith doesn't prove the Resurrection or that Christianity is true. It is part of a cumulative case that helps establish the sincerity of the apostles. It shows they weren't liars and that they truly believed Jesus had appeared to them after his death.

The perspective I often hear is, "Well, these men were willing to die for a lie. Many people have done that. So what does it prove?"

Modern martyrs die for what they sincerely believe is true, but their beliefs are rooted in testimony passed on to them from others. For instance, the Muslim terrorists who attacked the Twin Towers on September 11, 2001, did not witness any miracles of Muhammad firsthand. In fact, they lived over thirteen centuries after Muhammad. No doubt the Muslim radicals were sincere, but their convictions were rooted in beliefs passed on for centuries. They did not know Muhammad personally, hear his teachings firsthand, or witness him performing any miracles, such as walking on water, healing the blind, or rising from the dead.

There is a massive difference between willingly dying for the sake of the religious ideas accepted from the testimony of others (as in the case of the September 11 terrorists) and willingly dying for the proclamation of a faith based on one's own eyewitness account (the apostles). The deaths of the nineteen terrorists provide no more credibility for their beliefs than our sacrifices would provide for our beliefs. Our martyrdoms would show we really believed it, but unlike the apostles, we were not eyewitnesses to the resurrection of Jesus.

Let's look at several factors that will help us understand why the apostles could not have been honestly mistaken about what they proclaimed.

They Were Eyewitnesses

As we have seen, the apostles wrote and other disciples spoke as actual eyewitnesses to the events they described. They did not report material secondhand but wrote about what they had personally seen and heard. John says he personally "has borne witness" and that "he is telling the truth" (John 19:35, ESV). This raises an important question: Why can we trust their testimony? One reason is because they were with Jesus from the start of his ministry. In Acts 1:21-22, Luke cites the apostles' criteria for choosing a replacement for Judas: "So one of the men who have accompanied us during all the time that the Lord Jesus went in and out among us, beginning from the baptism of John until the day when he was taken up from us—one of these men must become with us a witness to his resurrection" (ESV). The apostles were with Jesus from the beginning *and* were witnesses of his resurrection.

This is the same message Jesus gave directly to the apostles before his arrest: "You also will bear witness, *because you have been with me from the beginning*" (John 15:27, ESV, emphasis added). According to New Testament scholar Richard Bauckham in his book *Jesus and the Eyewitnesses*, the early church placed special importance on the testimony of the disciples because they had been with Jesus at his baptism, when his ministry began, to his post-resurrection appearances.[1] It seems to have been widely known in the early church that the apostles were eyewitnesses to the ministry and appearances of Jesus and that they served as personal witnesses to his life, teachings, and resurrection.

> **What do you think?**
> *Is there anything or anyone that you would die for? Why do you feel that way?*

Is there any further evidence that we can trust their accounts? Yes, we can see if the *internal* claims are supported *externally*. The Gospel of John emphasizes locations and consistently gets incidental details right about them. For example, John correctly cites that traveling from the city of

Cana, the town where Jesus turned water to wine, to the Sea of Galilee involves going *downhill* (see John 2:12). The Sea of Galilee is actually below sea level. This is an unnecessary detail that John naturally (and correctly) includes in his narrative.[2] But there's more. Archaeologists have discovered a location in the vicinity of Cana where stone pots were made, which corresponds with the "six stone water jars" described in John 2:6 that Jesus used to hold the wine.[3]

> **What do you think?**
>
> Have you ever been an eyewitness to something and later were asked to tell what you saw? Did people believe you? What makes someone a credible witness?

This is only one example of the author of John getting incidental details right, but it illustrates the kinds of patterns we see in all four Gospels. Our earliest accounts consistently testify that the apostles saw the risen Jesus, offered their personal testimonies, and these testimonies are often confirmed in the historical record. The Gospels give the kinds of details we would expect from genuine eyewitness accounts. As the apostle Peter said, the apostles did not invent clever stories but proclaimed what they saw *with their own eyes* (see 2 Peter 1:16).

They Had to Be Convinced

The apostles thought that when Jesus died, it was all over. When he was arrested, they ran and hid (see Mark 14:50). When they were told the tomb was empty, they did not at first believe it (see Luke 24:11). Only after ample and convincing evidence did they believe. Thomas said he wouldn't believe Christ was raised from the dead until he had put his finger into Christ's wounds. Thomas was willing to suffer for Jesus and may have died a martyr's death. Was he deceived? He bet his life that he was not.

What do you think?

For the most part, Jesus' siblings were resistant to what he was doing and saying. Traditionally, family members are often the most resistant to a change in a family member. Why do you think that is?

Peter denied his Lord several times during Christ's trial and finally deserted him. But something turned this coward around. A short time after Christ's crucifixion and burial, Peter showed up in Jerusalem preaching boldly, under the threat of death, that Jesus was the Christ and had been resurrected. Finally, Peter died as a martyr. What could have turned this terrified deserter into such a bold lion for Jesus? Why was Peter suddenly willing to die for him? Was the apostle deceived? Hardly. I believe it was a combination of two things. First, Peter and the apostles were filled by the Holy Spirit. Second, we read in 1 Corinthians 15:5 that after Christ's resurrection, "he was seen by Peter." Peter witnessed his Lord's resurrection, and he believed—to the extent that he was willing to die for his belief. He knew Jesus had conquered the grave and that he would too.

The classic example of a man convinced against his will was James, the brother of Jesus. Although James wasn't one of the original Twelve (see Matthew 10:2-4), he became the head of the church in Jerusalem and was later recognized as an apostle (see Galatians 1:19), along with Paul and Barnabas (see Acts 14:14). While Jesus was growing up and engaged in his ministry, James didn't believe that his brother was the Son of God (see John 7:5). No doubt James participated with his brothers in mocking Jesus, possibly saying things such as "You want people to believe in you? Why don't you go up to Jerusalem and put on a big show with all your miracles and healings?" James must have felt humiliated that his brother was bringing shame and ridicule on the family name with all his wild claims: "I am the way, the truth, and the life. No one can come to the Father except through me" (John 14:6); "I am the vine; you are the branches" (John 15:5); "I am the good shepherd; I know my own sheep, and they know me" (John 10:14). What would you think if your brother went around town saying such things?

But something happened to James. After Jesus was crucified and buried, James was preaching in Jerusalem. His message was that Jesus died for our sins and was resurrected and is alive. Eventually James became a leading figure in the Jerusalem church and was stoned to death on orders from Ananias, the high priest.[4] What could have changed James from an embarrassed scoffer to a man willing to die for his brother's deity? Was James deceived? Not likely. The most reasonable explanation is what we read in 1 Corinthians 15:7: "Then [after Christ's resurrection] he was seen by James." James saw the resurrected Christ and believed.

J. P. Moreland, professor of philosophy at the Talbot School of Theology, explains the significance of the fact that

> **What could have changed James from an embarrassed scoffer to a man willing to die for his brother's deity? James saw the resurrected Christ and believed.**

James, the brother of Jesus, eventually came to believe in Jesus as the Messiah:

> The gospels tell us Jesus' family, including James, were embarrassed by what he was claiming to be. They didn't believe in him; they confronted him. In ancient Judaism it was highly embarrassing for a rabbi's family not to accept him. Therefore, the gospel writers would have no motive for fabricating this skepticism if it weren't true. Later the historian Josephus tells us that James, the brother of Jesus, who was the leader of the Jerusalem church, was stoned to death because of his belief in his brother. Why did James's life change? Paul tells us: the resurrected Jesus appeared to him. There's no other explanation.[5]

If the Resurrection were a lie, the apostles would have known it. Were they perpetuating a colossal hoax? Such a possibility is inconsistent with what we know about the moral quality of their lives. They personally condemned lying and stressed honesty. They encouraged people to know the truth. Historian Edward Gibbon, in his famous work *The History of the Decline and Fall of the Roman Empire*, gives the "purer but austere morality of the first Christians" as one of the five reasons for the rapid success of Christianity.[6] Michael Green, senior research fellow at Wycliffe Hall, Oxford University, observes that the Resurrection

> was the belief that turned heartbroken followers of a crucified rabbi into the courageous witnesses

and martyrs of the early church. This was the one belief that separated the followers of Jesus from the Jews and turned them into the community of the resurrection. You could imprison them, flog them, kill them, but you could not make them deny their conviction that "on the third day he rose again."[7]

Let's consider one objection: if the apostolic witness about the Resurrection was a lie, then wouldn't we expect them to also lie about not believing it at first? This objection might seem true, but it still doesn't explain how the apostles were first convinced to believe that a crucified criminal was their savior. Crucifixion was the most dishonorable death imaginable. It was a shameful death, which raises a troubling question: Why would the apostles invent *this* story about Jesus? Why not give him an honorable death? Rather than believing the apostles invented the story of his death and resurrection, it makes far more sense to take them at their word: they were witnesses of the risen Jesus. *That's* what convinced them.

They Became Courageous

The bold conduct of the apostles after they were convinced of the Resurrection makes it highly unlikely that it was all a fraud. They became courageous almost overnight. After the Resurrection, Peter—who had denied Christ—stood up even at the threat of death and proclaimed that Jesus was alive. The authorities arrested the followers of Christ and beat them, yet they were soon back on the street, speaking out about Jesus (see Acts 5:40-42). Their friends noticed their buoyancy, and their enemies noticed their courage. Remember that the apostles did not confine their boldness to obscure towns. They preached in Jerusalem, the very place Jesus was crucified.

Jesus' followers would not likely have faced torture and death unless they were convinced of his resurrection. The willingness of all the apostles to proclaim the Resurrection amid threats is remarkable.

Jesus' followers would not likely have faced torture and death unless they were convinced of his resurrection. The willingness of all the apostles to proclaim the Resurrection amid threats, beatings, and imprisonment is remarkable. If they were deceivers, it's hard to explain why at least one of them didn't abandon the faith for a more comfortable life.

Blaise Pascal, the French philosopher, writes,

The allegation that the Apostles were imposters is quite absurd. Let us follow the charge to its logical conclusion. Let us picture those twelve men, meeting after the death of Christ, and entering into conspiracy to say that He has risen. That would have constituted an attack upon both the civil and the religious authorities. The heart of man is strangely given to fickleness and change; it is swayed by promises, tempted by material things. If any one of those men had yielded to temptations so alluring, or given way to the more compelling arguments of prison, torture, they would have all been lost.[8]

At the conclusion of his academic research on the apostles, my son (Sean) sums up the significance of their sufferings:

> The apostles proclaimed the risen Jesus to skeptical and antagonistic audiences with full knowledge they would likely suffer and die for their beliefs. All the apostles suffered and were "ready to be put to death," and we have good reason to believe some of them actually faced execution. There is no evidence they ever wavered. Their convictions were not based on secondhand testimony, but personal experience with the risen Jesus, whom they truly believed was the risen Messiah, banking their lives on it. It is difficult to imagine what more a group of ancient witnesses could have done to show greater depth of sincerity and commitment to the truth.[9]

One writer descriptively narrates the changes that occurred in the lives of the apostles:

> On the day of the crucifixion they were filled with sadness; on the first day of the week with gladness. At the crucifixion they were hopeless; on the first day of the week their hearts glowed with certainty and hope. When the message of the resurrection first came, they were incredulous and hard to be convinced, but once they became assured they never doubted again. What could account for the astonishing change in these men in so short a time? The mere removal of the body

from the grave could never have transformed their spirits and characters. Three days are not enough for a legend to spring up which would so affect them. Time is needed for a process of legendary growth. It is a psychological fact that demands a full explanation. Think of the character of the witnesses, men and women who gave the world the highest ethical teaching it has ever known, and who even on the testimony of their enemies lived it out in their lives. Think of the psychological absurdity of picturing a little band of defeated cowards cowering in an upper room one day and a few days later transformed into a company that no persecution could silence—and then attempting to attribute this dramatic change to nothing more convincing than a miserable fabrication they were trying to foist upon the world. That simply wouldn't make sense.[10]

Church historian Kenneth Scott Latourette writes,

The effects of the resurrection and the coming of the Holy Spirit upon the disciples were . . . of major importance. From discouraged, disillusioned men and women who sadly looked back upon the days when they had hoped that Jesus "was he who should redeem Israel," they were made over into a company of enthusiastic witnesses.[11]

N. T. Wright, former professor of New Testament studies at Oxford University in England, explains that "far and away the best explanation for the early Christian mutation within Jewish resurrection-belief is that two things had happened. First, Jesus' tomb was found to be empty. Second, several people, including at least one, and perhaps more, who had not previously been followers of Jesus, claimed to have seen him alive."[12]

What do you think?

Do you admire people who are willing to die or have died for a cause? What attracts you to them? What scares you about them? Is there anything you can learn from them?

The steadfastness of the apostles even with the threat of death cannot be explained away. Two of the most important apostles are Peter and Paul. The author of 1 Clement, a letter written to Corinth from Rome around AD 95, confirms that both Peter and Paul were persecuted to the point of death (see 1 Clement 5:1-7). They sealed their witness to Jesus with their blood.

Harvard law professor Simon Greenleaf, a man who lectured for years on how to break down a witness and determine whether he was lying, concludes, "The annals of military warfare afford scarcely an example of the like heroic constancy, patience, and unflinching courage. They had every possible motive to review carefully the grounds of their faith, and the evidence of the great facts and truths which they asserted."[13]

There is little historical doubt that Christianity began in Jerusalem within weeks after the death of Jesus, and in the presence of hostile witnesses. This matters because, as philosopher William Lane Craig has observed, "The site of Jesus' tomb was known to Christians and Jews alike. So if it weren't empty, it would be impossible for a movement founded on belief in the Resurrection to have come into existence in the same city where this man had been publicly executed and buried."[14]

The apostles were willing to die for the veracity of what they were proclaiming. I believe I can trust their testimony more than that of most people I meet today, who are unwilling to suffer for what they believe, not to mention die for it.

CHAPTER 7

What Good Is a Dead Messiah?

Many people have died for causes they believe in.

In the 1960s many Buddhists burned themselves to death in order to bring world attention to injustices in Southeast Asia. In the early seventies a San Diego student burned himself to death protesting the Vietnam War. On September 11, 2001, several Muslim extremists hijacked airliners and crashed them into the World Trade Center towers and the Pentagon to inflict damage on a nation they considered an enemy to their religion.

The apostles thought they had a good cause to die for, but they were stunned and disillusioned when that good cause died on the cross. They believed Jesus to be the Messiah. They didn't think he could die. They were convinced that he was the one to set up the Kingdom of God and to rule over the people of Israel. His death shattered their hopes (see Luke 24:21).

In order to understand the apostles' relationship to

Christ and why the Cross was so incomprehensible to them, you must grasp the national attitude about the Messiah at the time of Christ. His life and teachings were in tremendous conflict with the Jewish messianic understanding of that day. From childhood a Jew was taught that when the Messiah came, he would be a victorious, reigning political leader. He would free the Jews from bondage to the Romans and restore Israel to its rightful place as an independent nation that would shine like a beacon to all the world. A suffering Messiah was "completely foreign to the Jewish conception of messiahship."[1]

What do you think?

Have you ever heard of someone having a messiah complex? What does that mean? How does Jesus' behavior differ from what people expect from a messiah?

Professor E. F. Scott, professor of biblical theology at Union Theological Seminary, gives his account of the expectant atmosphere at the time of Christ:

> The period was one of intense excitement. The religious leaders found it almost impossible to restrain the ardour of the people, who were waiting everywhere for the appearance of the promised Deliverer. This mood of expectancy had no doubt been heightened by the events of recent history.
>
> For more than a generation past, the Romans had been encroaching on Jewish freedom, and their measures of repression had stirred the spirit of patriotism to fiercer life. The dream of a miraculous deliverance, and of a Messianic king

who would effect it, assumed a new meaning in that critical time; but in itself it was nothing new. Behind the ferment of which we have evidence In the Gospels, we can discern a long period of growing anticipation.

To the people at large the Messiah remained what he had been to Isaiah and his contemporaries—the Son of David who would bring victory and prosperity to the Jewish nation. In the light of the Gospel references it can hardly be doubted that the popular conception of the Messiah was mainly national and political.[2]

Jewish scholar Joseph Klausner writes, "The Messiah became more and more not only a preeminent political ruler but also a man of preeminent moral qualities."[3]

Jacob Gartenhaus, founder of the International Board of Jewish Missions, reflects the prevailing Jewish beliefs in the time of Christ: "The Jews awaited the Messiah as the one who would deliver them from Roman oppression. . . . The messianic hope was basically for a national liberation."[4]

The *Jewish Encyclopedia* states that the Jews "yearned for the promised deliverer of the house of David, who would free them from the yoke of the hated foreign usurper, would put an end to the impious Roman rule, and would establish His own reign of peace and justice in its place."[5]

At that time the Jews were taking refuge in the promised Messiah. The apostles held the same beliefs as the people around them, which is why they did not at all welcome Jesus' grave predictions about being crucified (see Luke 9:22). As Scottish New Testament professor A. B. Bruce observes, there "seems to have been the hope that He had taken too gloomy a view of the situation, and that His apprehensions would turn out groundless . . . a crucified Christ was a scandal and a contradiction to the apostles; quite as much as it continued to be to the majority of the Jewish people after the Lord had ascended to glory."[6]

Alfred Edersheim, once Grinfield Lecturer on the Septuagint at Oxford University, is right in concluding that "the most unlike thing to Christ were his times."[7] The reality of the person was utterly at odds with the heightened expectations of the day.

We can easily see in the New Testament the apostles' attitude toward Christ. Many aspects of Jesus' life and ministry contrasted with their expectation of a reigning Messiah. After Jesus told them that he had to go to Jerusalem and suffer, James and John ignored the gloomy prediction and asked him to promise that in his Kingdom they could sit at his right and his left (see Mark 10:32-38). What type of Messiah were they thinking of—a suffering, crucified Messiah? No. They saw Jesus as a political ruler. He indicated that they had misunderstood what he had to do; they didn't know what they were asking. When he explicitly predicted his suffering and crucifixion, the idea was so foreign to the apostles' mindset that they couldn't figure out what he meant (see Luke 18:31-34).

We can easily see in the New Testament the apostles' attitude toward Christ. Many aspects of Jesus' life and ministry contrasted with their expectation of a reigning Messiah.

Because of their background and training in the general Jewish messianic expectation, they thought they were in on a good thing. Then came Calvary. All hopes that Jesus was their Messiah died on the cross. A victorious savior couldn't possibly be put to death in such a humiliating and dishonorable fashion. And they were not expecting a crucified Messiah. According to Deuteronomy 21:23, the one who hangs on a tree is cursed. In their minds, crucifixion meant shame and defeat, not victory. They returned to their homes, discouraged that all those years with Jesus had been wasted.

What do you think?

Have any of your ideas about Jesus been shattered? Confirmed? Why do you think the disciples had so much difficulty knowing exactly who he was?

But a few weeks after the Crucifixion, in spite of their former doubts, the disciples were in Jerusalem, proclaiming Jesus as Savior and Lord, the Messiah of the Jews. The only reasonable explanation I can see for this change is what I read in 1 Corinthians 15:5: "He was seen by Peter and then by the Twelve [apostles]." What else could have caused the despondent disciples to go out and suffer and die for a crucified Messiah? Jesus "appeared to the apostles from time to time, and he proved to them in many ways that he was actually alive. And he talked to them about the Kingdom of God" (Acts 1:3). This was the conclusion of Pinchas Lapide, a Jewish scholar who wrote a book on the resurrection of Jesus:

> When this scared, frightened band of apostles which
> was just about to throw away everything in order
> to flee in despair to Galilee; when these peasants,
> shepherds, and fishermen, who betrayed and denied
> their master and failed him so miserably, suddenly

could be changed overnight into a confident mission society, convinced of salvation and able to work with much more success after Easter than before, then no vision or hallucination is sufficient to explain such a revolutionary transformation.[8]

These men learned the truth about Jesus' identity as the Messiah. Unfortunately, most of the Messiah's own people misunderstood. Their national patriotism had led them to look only for a savior for their own nation. What came instead was a Messiah to save the world. A Messiah who would save not merely one nation from political oppression but all of humanity from the eternal consequences of sin. The apostles' vision had been too small. Suddenly they saw the larger truth.

The Jews' national patriotism had led them to look only for a savior for their own nation. What came instead was a Messiah to save all of humanity from the eternal consequences of sin.

Yes, many people have died for a good cause, but the good cause of the apostles had died on the cross. At least, that is what they first thought. Only their contact with Christ after the Resurrection convinced these men that he was indeed the Messiah. To this they testified not only with their lips and lives but also with their deaths.

CHAPTER 8

Did You Hear What Happened to Saul?

Jack, a Christian friend of mine who has spoken at many universities, arrived at a campus one morning to discover that the students had arranged for him to have a public discussion that night with the "university atheist." His opponent was an eloquent philosophy professor who was extremely antagonistic to Christianity. Jack was to speak first. He discussed various proofs for the resurrection of Jesus as well as the conversion of the apostle Paul. Then he gave his personal testimony about how Christ had changed his life when he was a university student.

When the philosophy professor got up to speak, he was quite nervous. He couldn't refute the evidence for the Resurrection or Jack's personal testimony, so he attacked the apostle Paul's radical conversion to Christianity. He used the argument that "people can often become so psychologically involved in what they're combating that they end up embracing it."

My friend smiled gently and responded, "You'd better be careful, sir, or you're liable to become a Christian."

The story of the apostle Paul is one of the most influential testimonies to Christianity. Saul of Tarsus, perhaps the most rabid antagonist of early Christianity, became the apostle Paul, the most energetic and influential spokesman for the new movement. In his letter to the Philippians, he described his former self as "circumcised on the eighth day, of the people of Israel, of the tribe of Benjamin, a Hebrew of Hebrews; as to the law, a Pharisee; as to zeal, a persecutor of the church; as to righteousness under the law, blameless" (3:5-6, ESV).

His birth in Tarsus gave him exposure to the most advanced learning of his day. Tarsus was a university city known for its Stoic philosophers and culture. Strabo, the Greek geographer, praised Tarsus for its avid interest in education and philosophy.

Paul, like his father, possessed Roman citizenship, a high privilege. Paul seemed to be well-versed in Hellenistic culture and thought. He had great command of the Greek language and displayed superb dialectic skill. He often quoted from less familiar poets and philosophers. In one of his speeches Paul quotes and alludes to Epimenides, Aratus, and Cleanthes: "In him we live and move and exist. As some of your own poets have said, 'We are his offspring'"

> **What do you think?**
>
> *The apostle Paul completely reversed his beliefs about Jesus after experiencing a life-transforming encounter with him. Have you ever seen that kind of transformation in anyone? Have you ever experienced it yourself?*

(Acts 17:28). In one of his letters, Paul quotes Menander: "Don't be fooled by those who say such things, for 'bad company corrupts good character'" (1 Corinthians 15:33). In a later letter to Titus, Paul again quotes Epimenides: "One of their own men, a prophet from Crete, has said about them, 'The people of Crete are all liars, cruel animals, and lazy gluttons'" (Titus 1:12).

Paul's education was Jewish and took place under the strict doctrines of the Pharisees. When Paul was about age fourteen, he was sent to study under Gamaliel, the grandson of Hillel, one of the great rabbis of the time. Paul asserted that he was not only a Pharisee but also the son of Pharisees (see Acts 23:6). He could boast, "I was far ahead of my fellow Jews in my zeal for the traditions of my ancestors" (Galatians 1:14).

To understand Paul's conversion, it is necessary to see why he was so vehemently anti-Christian. It was his devotion to the Jewish law that triggered his adamant opposition to Christ and the early church. Paul's "offense with the Christian message was not," as French theologian Jacques Dupont writes, "with the affirmation of Jesus' messiahship [but] . . . with the attributing to Jesus of a saving role which robbed the law of all its value in the purpose of salvation. . . . [Paul was] violently hostile to the Christian faith because of the importance which he attached to the law as a way of salvation."[1]

The members of the new sect of Judaism calling themselves Christians struck at the essence of Paul's Jewish training and rabbinic studies. As a practicing Jew, he would have believed that the reason Israel was subject to Rome was because of their failure to follow the law. Straying from the law could only bring down greater

The members of the new sect of Judaism calling themselves Christians struck at the essence of Paul's Jewish training and rabbinic studies. He became passionate about exterminating this dangerous movement.

wrath from God. He saw it as his obligation to stop this new heretical sect. Thus, Paul became passionate about exterminating this danger-ous movement (see Galatians 1:13). He began pursuing Christians and putting them to death (see Acts 26:9-11). Paul single-mindedly began to destroy the church (see Acts 8:3). He set out for Damascus with documents authorizing him to seize the followers of Jesus and bring them back to face trial.

Then something happened to Paul:

> Meanwhile, Saul [later known as Paul] was uttering threats with every breath and was eager to kill the Lord's followers. So he went to the high priest. He requested letters addressed to the synagogues in Damascus, asking for their cooperation in the arrest of any followers of the Way [another way to say Christians] he found there. He wanted to bring them—both men and women—back to Jerusalem in chains.
>
> As he was approaching Damascus on this mission, a light from heaven suddenly shone down around him. He fell to the ground and heard a voice saying to him, "Saul! Saul! Why are you persecuting me?"
>
> "Who are you, lord?" Saul asked.

And the voice replied, "I am Jesus, the one you are persecuting! Now get up and go into the city, and you will be told what you must do."

The men with Saul stood speechless, for they heard the sound of someone's voice but saw no one! Saul picked himself up off the ground, but when he opened his eyes he was blind. So his companions led him by the hand to Damascus. He remained there blind for three days and did not eat or drink.

Now there was a believer in Damascus named Ananias. The Lord spoke to him in a vision, calling, "Ananias!"

"Yes, Lord!" he replied.

The Lord said, "Go over to Straight Street, to the house of Judas. When you get there, ask for a man from Tarsus named Saul. He is praying to me right now. I have shown him a vision of a man named Ananias coming in and laying his hands on him so he can see again."

ACTS 9:1-12

As we read on, we can see why Christians feared Paul:

"But Lord," exclaimed Ananias, "I've heard many people talk about the terrible things this man has done to the believers in Jerusalem! And he is authorized by the leading priests to arrest everyone who calls upon your name."

But the Lord said, "Go, for Saul is my chosen instrument to take my message to the Gentiles and to kings, as well as to the people of Israel.

And I will show him how much he must suffer for my name's sake."

So Ananias went and found Saul. He laid his hands on him and said, "Brother Saul, the Lord Jesus, who appeared to you on the road, has sent me so that you might regain your sight and be filled with the Holy Spirit." Instantly something like scales fell from Saul's eyes, and he regained his sight. Then he got up and was baptized. Afterward he ate some food and regained his strength.

ACTS 9:13-19

What do you think?

Why do you think Paul's conversion had to be so dramatic? How did God's plan for Paul's life differ from Paul's own plan for his life?

As a result of this experience, Paul considered himself a witness to the resurrected Christ. He later wrote, "Haven't I seen Jesus our Lord with my own eyes?" (1 Corinthians 9:1). He compared Christ's appearance to him with Christ's post-resurrection appearances to the other apostles: "Last of all . . . I also saw him" (1 Corinthians 15:8).

Not only did Paul see Jesus, but he saw him in an irresistible way. He didn't proclaim the gospel out of choice but from necessity: "Preaching the Good News is not something I can boast about. I am compelled by God to do it" (1 Corinthians 9:16).

Notice that Paul's encounter with Jesus and his subsequent conversion were sudden and unexpected: "A very bright light from heaven suddenly shone down around me" (Acts 22:6). He had no idea who this heavenly person could be. When the voice announced that he was Jesus of Nazareth, Paul was astonished and began to tremble.

We might be tempted to dismiss Paul's testimony because, after all, there are many examples of radical conversions to another faith. But New Testament scholar Michael Licona draws an important distinction: "Today we might believe that Jesus rose from the dead based on secondary evidence, trusting Paul and the disciples who saw the risen Jesus. But for Paul, his experience came from primary evidence: he had an experience he perceived as the risen Jesus, who had appeared directly to him."[2]

Some have suggested that Paul only thought he had an experience of Jesus but really suffered from hallucinations. The challenge with this diagnosis is that Paul's own story includes not just a vision of Jesus but others around him experiencing a heavenly encounter as well (see Acts 22:9). Plus, if Paul suffered from hallucinations, he would have likely known about his condition and used it to explain away his episode with Jesus. We might not know all the details or psychology of what happened to Paul on the road to Damascus, but we do know this: the experience utterly overturned every area of his life.

First, Paul's character was radically transformed. According to Dr. Douglas Campbell, professor of New Testament at Duke Divinity School, "This must have been a humbling moment, and I doubt that Paul ever forgot

We might not know all the details or psychology of what happened to Paul on the road to Damascus, but we do know this: the experience utterly overturned every area of his life.

the way that his own zeal had misled him. He now realized that in and of himself he had nothing to offer God and was in fact deeply twisted in his understanding of his Lord. The God revealed in Jesus Christ judged his activity and exposed its corruption. The result was a Paul who speaks very much like a recovering substance abuser. He was able to look back on his previous life with a mind clarified by this revelation and see where his previous activity, which looked entirely reasonable if not praiseworthy at the time, was profoundly distorted."[3]

Second, Paul's relationship with the followers of Jesus was transformed. They were no longer afraid of him. Paul "stayed with the believers in Damascus for a few days" (Acts 9:19). And when he went to meet the other apostles, they accepted him (see verses 27-28).

Third, Paul's message was transformed. Though he still loved his Jewish heritage, he had changed from a bitter antagonist to a determined protagonist of the Christian faith. He immediately began preaching about Jesus in the synagogues, claiming that Jesus is the Son of God (see Acts 9:20). His intellectual convictions had changed. His experience compelled him to acknowledge that Jesus was the Messiah, in direct conflict with the Pharisees' messianic ideas. His new perspective of Christ meant a total revolution in his thinking. Jacques Dupont acutely observes that after Paul "had passionately denied that a crucified man could be the Messiah, he came to grant that Jesus was indeed the Messiah, and, as a consequence, rethought all his messianic ideas."[4]

Also, Paul could now understand that Christ's death on the cross, which appeared to be a curse of God and a deplorable ending to a life, was actually God reconciling the world to himself through Christ. Paul came to understand that through the Crucifixion, Christ took the curse of sin on himself for us (see Galatians 3:13) and that God "made Christ, who never sinned, to be the offering for our sin, so that we could be made right with God through Christ" (2 Corinthians 5:21). Instead of seeing the death of Christ as a defeat, he saw it as a great victory, completed by the Resurrection. The Cross was no longer a stumbling block but the essence of God's messianic redemption. Paul's missionary preaching can be summarized as "he explained the prophecies and proved that the Messiah must suffer and rise from the dead. He said, 'This Jesus I'm telling you about is the Messiah'" (Acts 17:3).

Fourth, Paul's mission was transformed. He was changed from a hater of the Gentiles to a missionary to the Gentiles. He was changed from a Jewish radical to a missionary to non-Jews. As a Jew and a Pharisee, Paul looked down on the Gentiles as inferior to God's chosen people. The Damascus experience changed him into a dedicated apostle with his life's mission focused on preaching to the Gentiles. Paul saw that the Christ who appeared to him was indeed the Savior for all people. Paul went from being an orthodox Pharisee, whose mission was to preserve strict Judaism, to being an evangelist of the new, radical sect that he had so violently opposed. The change in him was so profound that "all who heard him were amazed. 'Isn't this the same man who caused

Instead of seeing the death of Christ as a defeat, he saw it as a great victory, completed by the Resurrection. The Cross was the essence of God's messianic redemption.

such devastation among Jesus' followers in Jerusalem?' they asked. 'And didn't he come here to arrest them and take them in chains to the leading priests?' Saul's preaching became more and more powerful, and the Jews in Damascus couldn't refute his proofs that Jesus was indeed the Messiah" (Acts 9:21-22).

Historian Philip Schaff states, "The conversion of Paul marks not only a turning-point in his personal history, but also an important epoch in the history of the apostolic church, and consequently in the history of mankind. It was the most fruitful event since the miracle of Pentecost, and secured the universal victory of Christianity."[5]

During lunch one day at the University of Houston, I sat down next to a student. As we discussed Christianity, he made the statement that there was no historical evidence for Christianity or Christ. I asked him why he thought that. He was a history major, and one of his textbooks was a Roman history text that contained a chapter dealing with the apostle Paul and Christianity. The student had read the chapter and found that it started by describing the life of Saul of Tarsus and ended describing the life of Paul the apostle. The book stated that what caused the change was not clear. I turned to the book of Acts and explained Christ's post-resurrection appearance to Paul. The student saw immediately that this was the most logical explanation for Paul's radical conversion. This bit of missing evidence made the pieces fall into place for this young man. Later he became a Christian.

Elias Andrews, principal of Queens Theological College, comments, "Many have found in the radical transformation of this 'Pharisee of the Pharisees' the most convincing evidence of the truth and the power of the religion to which he was converted, as well as the ultimate worth and place of the Person of Christ."[6]

Archibald McBride, a professor at the University of Aberdeen, writes of Paul, "Beside his achievements . . . the achievements of Alexander and Napoleon pale into insignificance."[7]

Paul states again and again that the living, resurrected Jesus had transformed his life. He was so convinced of Christ's resurrection from the dead that he was willing to suffer greatly for his service to Christ. In his second letter to the Corinthians, Paul catalogues what he endured:

> Five times I received at the hands of the Jews the forty lashes less one. Three times I was beaten with rods. Once I was stoned. Three times I was shipwrecked; a night and a day I was adrift at sea; on frequent journeys, in danger from rivers, danger from robbers, danger from my own people, danger from Gentiles, danger in the city, danger in the wilderness, danger at sea, danger from false brothers; in toil and hardship, through many a sleepless night, in hunger and thirst, often without food, in cold and exposure. And, apart from other things, there is the daily pressure on me of my anxiety for all the churches.
>
> 2 CORINTHIANS 11:24-28, ESV

As my son Sean documents in his research on the apostles, early church history consistently affirms that Paul died as a martyr. He paid the ultimate price for his belief that Jesus had risen from the grave.

Two Oxford-educated friends, author Gilbert West and statesman Lord George Lyttelton, were determined to destroy the basis of the Christian faith. West was going to demonstrate the fallacy of the Resurrection, and Lyttelton was going to prove that Saul of Tarsus never converted to Christianity. Both men came to a complete turnaround in their positions and became ardent followers of Jesus. Lord Lyttelton writes, "The conversion and apostleship of Saint Paul alone, duly considered, was of itself a demonstration sufficient to prove Christianity to be a Divine Revelation."[8] He concludes that if Paul's twenty-five years of suffering and service for Christ was a reality, then his conversion was true, for everything he did began with that sudden change. And if Paul's conversion was true, then Jesus Christ rose from the dead, for everything Paul was and did he attributed to his witnessing the risen Christ.

CHAPTER 9

Can You Keep a Good Man Down?

A student at the University of Uruguay asked me, "Professor McDowell, why couldn't you find some way to refute Christianity?"

I answered, "For a very simple reason. I was unable to explain away the fact that the resurrection of Jesus Christ was a real event in history."

After spending more than seven hundred hours studying this subject and thoroughly investigating its foundation, I concluded that the resurrection of Jesus Christ is either one of the most wicked, vicious, heartless hoaxes ever foisted on humanity, or it is the most important fact in history.

The Resurrection takes the question "Is Christianity valid?" out of the realm of philosophy and puts it in the realm of history. Does Christianity have a solid historical basis? Is sufficient evidence available to warrant belief in the Resurrection?

Here are some of the issues and claims relevant to the question: Jesus of Nazareth, a Jewish prophet who claimed to be the Christ prophesied in the Jewish Scriptures, was arrested, judged to be a political criminal, and crucified.

The resurrection of Jesus Christ is either one of the most wicked, vicious, heartless hoaxes ever foisted on humanity, or it is the most important fact in history.

Three days after his death and burial, some women who went to his tomb found the body to be missing. Christ's disciples claimed that God had raised him from the dead and that he had appeared to them many times before ascending to heaven.

From this foundation, Christianity spread throughout the Roman Empire and has continued to exert great influence throughout the world through all subsequent centuries.

The big question is, Did the Resurrection actually happen?

The Death and Burial of Jesus

After Jesus was condemned to death, he was stripped of his clothing and was whipped, according to Roman custom, before crucifixion.

Alexander Metherell, who holds a medical degree from the University of Miami and a doctorate in engineering from the University of Bristol in England, made a detailed examination of Christ's whipping at the hands of the Romans. He explains the process:

The soldier would use a whip of braided leather thongs with metal balls woven into them. When the whip would strike the flesh, these balls would cause deep bruises or contusions, which would break open with further blows. And the whip had pieces of sharp bone as well, which would cut the flesh severely.

The back would be so shredded that part of the spine was sometimes exposed by the deep, deep cuts. The whipping would have gone all the way from the shoulders down to the back, the buttocks, and the back of the legs. It was just terrible. . . .

One physician who has studied Roman beatings said, "As the flogging continued, the lacerations would tear into the underlying skeletal muscles and produce quivering ribbons of bleeding flesh." A third-century historian by the name of Eusebius described flogging by saying, "The sufferer's veins were laid bare, and the very muscles, sinews, and bowels of the victim were open to exposure."

We know that many people would die from this kind of beating even before they could be crucified. At the least, the victim would experience tremendous pain and go into hypovolemic shock.[1]

Given the brutality of the whipping, as well as his subsequent crucifixion and being pierced by a soldier's spear, it is historically certain that Jesus was dead. Even critical scholars accept the death of Jesus. John Dominic Crossan,

What do you think?

Have you seen any movies about Jesus' life that included his death and resurrection, such as The Passion of the Christ? What went through your mind when you saw Christ's torture and crucifixion? Do you think he deserved what happened to him?

for example, has said that the death of Jesus by crucifixion "is as sure as anything historical can ever be."[2]

In accordance with Jewish burial customs, the body of Jesus was then wrapped in a linen cloth. About seventy-five pounds of aromatic spices, mixed together to form a gummy substance, were applied to the wrappings around the body (see John 19:39-40). After the body was placed in a solid rock tomb, an extremely large stone, weighing approximately two tons, was rolled by means of levers against the entrance (see Matthew 27:60).

A Roman guard of strictly disciplined men was stationed to watch the tomb. Fear of punishment among these men "produced flawless attention to duty, especially in the night watches."[3] This guard affixed on the tomb the Roman seal, a stamp of Roman power and authority.[4] The seal was meant to prevent vandalism. Anyone trying to move the stone from the tomb's entrance would have broken the seal and thus incurred the wrath of Roman law.

Yet in spite of the guard and the seal, the tomb was empty.

The Empty Tomb

The followers of Jesus claimed he had risen from the dead. They reported that he appeared to them over a period of forty days, showing himself to them by many convincing proofs (some versions of the Bible say "infallible proofs"; see, for example, Acts 1:3, NKJV). The apostle Paul said that Jesus appeared to more than five hundred of his followers at one time, the majority of whom were still alive and could confirm what he wrote (see 1 Corinthians 15:3-8).

Arthur Michael Ramsey, former archbishop of Canterbury, writes, "I believe in the Resurrection, partly because a series of facts are unaccountable without it."[5] The empty tomb was "too notorious to be denied."[6] German theologian Paul Althaus states that the claim of the Resurrection "could not have been maintained in Jerusalem for a single day, for a single hour, if the emptiness of the tomb had not been established as a fact for all concerned."[7]

Paul L. Maier concludes, "If all the evidence is weighed carefully and fairly, it is indeed justifiable, according to the canons of historical research, to conclude that [Jesus' tomb] was actually empty. . . . And no shred of evidence has yet been discovered in literary sources, epigraphy, or archaeology that would disprove this statement."[8]

Based on substantial historical evidence, Christians believe that Jesus was bodily resurrected in real time and space by the supernatural power of God. The difficulties in belief may be great, but the problems inherent in disbelief are even greater.

How can we explain the empty tomb?

Based on substantial historical evidence, Christians believe that Jesus was bodily resurrected in real time and space by the supernatural power of God. The difficulties in belief may be great, but the problems inherent in disbelief are even greater.

The situation at the tomb after the Resurrection is significant. The Roman seal was broken, which meant severe punishment for whoever broke it. The massive stone was moved not just from the entrance but from the entire sepulchre, looking as if it had been picked up and carried away. In antiquity, stones were sometimes rolled away from tombs so that graves could be robbed. But this was virtually impossible with guards present because of the penalties for guards who failed their duties. New Testament scholar Craig Keener reports, "Penalties for falling asleep on guard duty could be severe, and guards who claimed to have slept through the stealing of the body, yet suffered no harm, would sound very suspicious."[9] What were those penalties? Roman soldiers who fell asleep could be beaten, scourged, and banished from family and country. Guards who let a prisoner escape could be executed.[10] The guards had every incentive to protect the tomb and the body.

What do you think?

Have you ever been part of a group and something happened that involved all of you? Were your stories the same? How difficult is it to get everyone to tell the exact same story?

According to all four Gospels, the women came and found the tomb empty. They panicked and went back to tell the men. Peter and John ran to the tomb. John arrived first, but he didn't enter. He looked inside and saw the graveclothes, caved in a little, but empty. The body of Christ had passed right through them into a new existence. Let's face it: a sight like that would make anyone a believer.

Alternative Theories to the Resurrection

Many people have advanced alternate theories to explain the Resurrection. While alternative theories can account for *some* of the historical facts, besides the Resurrection, no theory accounts for *all* the known facts. In fact, the weaknesses of some of them actually help build confidence in the truth of the Resurrection.

The Wrong-Tomb Theory

A theory proposed by British biblical scholar Kirsopp Lake assumes that the women who reported the body missing had mistakenly gone to the wrong tomb that morning. If so, then the disciples who went to check the women's story must have gone to the wrong tomb as well. We can be certain, however, that the Jewish authorities, who had asked for that Roman guard to be stationed at the tomb to prevent the body from being stolen, would not have been mistaken about the location. The Roman guards would also not have been mistaken, for they were there. If a wrong tomb were involved, the Jewish authorities would have lost no time in producing the body from the proper tomb, thus effectively quenching for all time any rumor of a resurrection.

The Hallucination Theory

Another attempted explanation claims that the appearances of Jesus after the Resurrection were either illusions or hallucinations. One difficulty for this theory is that hallucinations are individual occurrences, and there is scant evidence for group hallucinations. A group hallucination is as unlikely as a group dream. And yet Jesus appeared to multiple groups, including the eleven disciples (see John 20; Luke 24:36-49), the women leaving the tomb (see Matthew 28:8-10), and the five hundred witnesses (see 1 Corinthians 15:6).

The hallucination theory also doesn't explain the conversion of Paul or the empty tomb. Besides, if the disciples were hallucinating, where was the actual body of Jesus, and why didn't those who opposed him produce it?

The Swoon Theory

Nineteenth-century German rationalist Karl Venturini popularized the swoon theory over two centuries ago, and it is sometimes suggested even today. It claims that Jesus didn't really die on the cross; he merely fainted from exhaustion and loss of blood. Everyone thought he was dead, but later he was resuscitated, and the disciples thought it to be a resurrection.

German theologian David Friedrich Strauss, himself no believer in the Resurrection, deals a death blow to any thought that Jesus could have revived from a swoon and launched the Christian movement:

> It is impossible that a being who had stolen half-dead out of the sepulcher, who crept about weak and ill, wanting medical treatment, who required bandaging, strengthening and indulgence, and who still at last yielded to his sufferings, could have given to the disciples the impression that he was a Conqueror over death and the grave, the Prince of Life, an impression which lay at the bottom of

their future ministry. Such a resuscitation could only have weakened the impression which He had made upon them in life and in death, at the most could only have given it an elegiac voice, but could by no possibility have changed their sorrow into enthusiasm, have elevated their reverence into worship.[11]

The Stolen-Body Theory

Another theory maintains that the disciples stole the body of Jesus while the guards slept. But this theory also falls apart. For one, the guards would have stopped the theft for reasons already mentioned (see Matthew 27:62-66). Additionally, the defeated mental state of the disciples makes a hard-hitting argument against it. Can we imagine that they suddenly became so brave and daring as to face a detachment of select soldiers at the tomb and steal the body? Apart from the filling of the Holy Spirit and the belief that Jesus had risen, they would have been in no mood to attempt anything like that.

Commenting on the proposition that the disciples stole Christ's body, J. N. D. Anderson says, "This would run totally contrary to all we know of them: their ethical teaching, the quality of their lives, their steadfastness in suffering and persecution. Nor would it begin to explain their dramatic transformation from dejected and dispirited escapists into witnesses whom no opposition could muzzle."[12]

Furthermore, if the disciples stole the body, then their testimony would have been rooted in lies. Are we to believe they intentionally fostered a lie to get themselves threatened, beaten, imprisoned, and possibly even martyred? Nonsense.

The Moved-Body Theory

Another theory says that the Romans, Jews, or some unknown authority moved Christ's body from the tomb. This explanation is no more reasonable than the stolen-body theory. If the authorities had the body in their possession or knew where it was, why didn't they explain that they had taken it, thus putting an effective end to the disciples' preaching of the Resurrection in Jerusalem? If the authorities had taken the body, why didn't they explain exactly where they had put it? Why didn't they recover the corpse, display it on a cart, and wheel it through the center of Jerusalem? Such an action would have utterly destroyed Christianity.

> **If the authorities had taken the body, why didn't they recover the corpse, display it on a cart, and wheel it through the center of Jerusalem? Such an action would have utterly destroyed Christianity.**

John Warwick Montgomery comments, "It passes the bounds of credibility that the early Christians could have manufactured such a tale and then preached it among those who might easily have refuted it simply by producing the body of Jesus."[13]

The Lost Tomb of Jesus Theory

This theory is also known as the Talpiot tomb theory because it is rooted in the idea that Jesus was reburied in the family tomb at Talpiot, five kilometers south of Jerusalem, after spending the Sabbath buried in Joseph of Arimathea's tomb. Thus, Joseph of Arimathea's tomb was only temporary, as Jesus' body was moved to complete the burial procedure. Even though this theory has garnered media attention due to the release of a book and film, it has been rejected by scholars. What is the evidence for rejecting it? For one, it contradicts the Gospel accounts of what happened to the body of Jesus. Second, the family of Jesus was not wealthy and would likely not have had a family tomb. If they did have one, it would have been in Galilee.[14] And finally, the names in the tomb, which overlap various Gospel figures, are common names of the time and not as suggestive as proponents think. There are even more severe problems that distinguished professor Craig Evans discusses in his article for the Biblical Archaeology Society titled "The Tomb of Jesus? Wrong on Every Count."[15]

This is why archaeologist Jodi Magness concludes that it is a "sensationalistic claim without any scientific basis or support."[16]

The Copycat Theory

"Nothing in Christianity is original" is one of the most commonly used lines of many skeptics today. In the late nineteenth and early twentieth centuries many scholars believed that the central claims of Christianity were plagiarized from Greco-Roman mystery religions. Jesus was considered another "dying and rising" god in the tradition of Osiris, Mithras, Adonis, and Dionysus. While this theory has experienced a surprising resurgence in popular circles, it faces near universal rejection by contemporary scholars. Here's why.

While parallels between Jesus and the mystery religions may appear striking on the surface, they collapse under

What do you think?

Can you think of any other possible naturalistic explanations for Jesus' resurrection? Does any other theory explain as many facts surrounding the events as his actual resurrection?

scrutiny. Osiris, for instance, is considered by many to be a dying and rising god from ancient Egypt. According to the myth, Osiris was killed by Seth and resuscitated by Isis. But rather than returning to the world in a resurrected body, Osiris became king of the underworld—hardly a parallel to the historical resurrection of Jesus. This is why Paul Rhodes Eddy and Gregory Boyd, authors of *The Jesus Legend*, conclude that "the differences between Christianity and the mystery religions are far more profound than any similarities. While there certainly are parallel terms used in early Christianity and the mystery religions, there is little evidence for parallel concepts."[17]

Unlike the historical Jesus, there is no evidence for the reliability of any of the alleged parallel stories in the mystery religions. Jesus of Nazareth ate, slept, performed miracles, died, and returned to life. These accounts are supported by reliable historical records. In contrast, the dying and rising gods of the mystery religions were timeless myths repeated annually with the changing seasons.

Swedish scholar T. N. D. Mettinger, professor of Hebrew Bible at Lund University, has examined the dying and rising gods hypothesis in depth. In *The Riddle of Resurrection*, Mettinger grants the existence of the myths of dying and rising gods in the ancient world, which, he admits, is a minority view. Yet his conclusion puts the nail in the coffin of the copycat theory:

There is, as far as I am aware, no prima facie evidence that the death and resurrection of Jesus is a mythological construct, drawing on the myths and rites of the dying and rising gods of the surrounding world. While studied with profit against the background of Jewish resurrection belief, the faith in the death and resurrection of Jesus retains its unique character in the history of religions. The riddle remains.[18]

Examining the Resurrection

Professor Thomas Arnold, author of the famous three-volume *History of Rome* and the chair of modern history at Oxford, was well acquainted with the value of evidence in determining historical facts. He says,

I have been used for many years to study the histories of other times, and to examine and weigh the evidence of those who have written about them, and I know of no one fact in the history of mankind which is proved by better and fuller evidence of every sort, to the understanding of a fair inquirer, than the great sign which God has given us that Christ died and rose again from the dead.[19]

British scholar Brooke Foss Westcott, divinity professor at Cambridge University, says, "Taking all the evidence together, it is not too much to say that there is no historic incident better or more variously supported than the resurrection of Christ. Nothing but the antecedent assumption that it must be false could have suggested the idea of deficiency in the proof of it."[20]

After carefully assessing the historical evidence for the resurrection of Jesus, Dr. William Lane Craig concludes that "the most reasonable historical explanation for the facts of the empty tomb, the resurrection appearances, and the origin of the Christian Way would therefore seem to be that Jesus rose from the dead."[21]

Simon Greenleaf was one of the greatest legal minds America has produced. He was the famous Royall Professor of Law at Harvard University and succeeded Justice Joseph Story as the Dane Professor of Law in the same university. While at Harvard, Greenleaf wrote a volume in which he examines the legal value of the apostles' testimony to the resurrection of Christ. He observes that it is impossible that the apostles "could have persisted in affirming the truths they had narrated, had not Jesus actually risen from the dead, and had they not known this fact as certainly as they knew any other fact."[22] Greenleaf concludes that the resurrection of Christ is one of the best-supported events in history according to the laws of legal evidence administered in courts of justice.

> It is impossible that the apostles "could have persisted in affirming the truths they had narrated, had not Jesus actually risen from the dead."

Sir Lionel Luckhoo is considered by many to be the world's most successful attorney after 245 consecutive murder acquittals. He served as a judge for the Supreme Court in Guyana and was knighted twice by Queen Elizabeth II. Yet he had no peace in his life until he became a follower of Jesus. "From that day my life changed," said Sir Lionel. "I moved from death to life, from darkness to light. I was born again."[23] This brilliant lawyer rigorously analyzed the historical facts of Christ's resurrection and finally declares,

> I have spent more than forty-two years as a defence trial lawyer appearing in many parts of the world. . . . I have been fortunate to secure a number of successes in jury trials and I say unequivocally the evidence for the resurrection of Jesus Christ is so overwhelming that it compels acceptance by proof which leaves absolutely no room for doubt.[24]

Frank Morison, another British lawyer, set out to refute the evidence for the Resurrection. He thought the life of Jesus was one of the most beautiful ever lived, but when it came to the Resurrection, Morison assumed someone had come along and tacked a myth onto the story. He planned to write an account of the last few days of Jesus, disregarding the Resurrection. The lawyer figured that an intelligent, rational approach to the story would completely discount such an event. However, when he applied his legal training to the facts, he had to change his mind. Instead of refuting the Resurrection, he eventually wrote the bestseller *Who Moved the Stone?* He titled the first chapter "The Book That Refused to Be Written." The rest of the book confirms decisively the validity of the evidence for Christ's resurrection.[25]

Most important of all, individual believers can experience the power of the risen Christ in their lives today. First of all, they can know their sins are forgiven (see

What do you think?

Is the fact that Jesus rose from the dead two thousand years ago relevant to you today? If so, how and why?

Luke 24:46-47; 1 Corinthians 15:3). Second, they can be assured of eternal life and their own resurrection from the grave (see 1 Corinthians 15:19-26). Third, they can be released from a meaningless and empty life and be transformed into new creatures in Jesus Christ (see John 10:10; 2 Corinthians 5:17).

What is your evaluation and decision? What do you think about the empty tomb? After examining the evidence from a judicial perspective, Lord Darling, former chief justice of England, concludes that "there exists such overwhelming evidence, positive and negative, factual and circumstantial, that no intelligent jury in the world could fail to bring in a verdict that the resurrection story is true."[26]

CHAPTER 10

Will the Real Messiah Please Stand Up?

Of all the credentials Jesus had to support his claims to be the Messiah and God's Son, one of the most profound is often overlooked: how his life fulfilled so many ancient prophecies. In this chapter I will deal with this astounding fact.

Over and over Jesus appealed to Old Testament prophecies to substantiate his claims. "Then Jesus took [the disciples] through the writings of Moses and all the prophets, explaining from all the Scriptures the things concerning himself" (Luke 24:27). Jesus said to his disciples, "When I was with you before, I told you that everything written about me in the law of Moses and the prophets and in the Psalms must be fulfilled" (verse 44). He said to the Jewish leaders, "If you really believed Moses, you would believe me, because he wrote about me" (John 5:46). And he told the people, "Your father Abraham rejoiced as he looked forward to my coming" (John 8:56).

The apostles and the New Testament writers also constantly appealed to fulfilled prophecy to substantiate the claims of Jesus as the Son of God, the Savior, and the Messiah:

> God was fulfilling what all the prophets had foretold about the Messiah—that he must suffer these things.
> ACTS 3:18

> As was Paul's custom, he went to the synagogue service, and for three Sabbaths in a row he used the Scriptures to reason with the people. He explained the prophecies and proved that the Messiah must suffer and rise from the dead. He said, "This Jesus I'm telling you about is the Messiah."
> ACTS 17:2-3

What do you think?

Do you think there is any difference between a prophecy and a prediction? Has anything ever been predicted about you at an early age that came true later? How is that different from the prophecies that Jesus fulfilled?

> I passed on to you what was most important and what had also been passed on to me. Christ died for our sins, just as the Scriptures said. He was buried, and he was raised from the dead on the third day, just as the Scriptures said.
> 1 CORINTHIANS 15:3-4

The Old Testament contains many types of events and characters that anticipate the coming of Jesus. For example, Joseph may be seen as a type of Jesus when he was falsely accused, sold for silver, and then became a deliverer of his people. Some consider these *backward*-facing prophetic anticipations that are clear after Jesus has arrived. The Old Testament also contains many *forward*-facing messianic prophecies that anticipate the arrival of the Messiah. It is helpful to look at these predictive prophecies fulfilled in Christ as his "address."

An Address in History

You've probably never realized the importance of your own name and address, yet these details set you apart from the more than eight billion other people who also inhabit this planet. With even greater detail, God wrote an "address" in history to single out his Son, the Messiah, the Savior of humanity, from anyone who has ever lived—past, present, or future. The specifics of this address can be found in the Old Testament, a document written over a period of a thousand years that contains multiple references and hints about the coming Messiah.

The likelihood of God's address matching up with one man is complicated by the fact that all the prophecies about the Messiah were recorded years before he was to appear. The books of the Old Testament were all written before Jesus was born. Some might suggest that these prophecies were written down after the time of Christ and fabricated to coincide with events in his life. Yet even critical scholars accept that there is a significant time gap between the writing of the Old Testament and the birth and life of Jesus.

Certainly God was writing an address in history that only his Messiah could fulfill. There have been many false messiahs. But only one man—Jesus Christ—had the credentials because he rose from the dead *and* fulfilled prophecy.

What are some of those messianic credentials? And what events had to precede and coincide with the appearance of God's Son?

To begin, we must go back to Genesis 3:15, where we find the first messianic prophecy in the Bible: "I will put enmity between you and the woman, and between your seed and her Seed; He shall bruise your head, and you shall bruise His heel" (NKJV). This prophecy could refer to only one man in all of Scripture. No one but Jesus, born of a virgin, could be referred to as the "seed" of a woman. All others born in history come from the seed of a man. Other translations make the same claim when they identify this conqueror of Satan to be the offspring of a woman, when in all other instances the Bible counts offspring through the line of the man. This offspring or "seed" of a woman will come into the world and destroy the works of Satan (bruise his head).

In Genesis 9 and 10 God narrowed down the address further. Noah had three sons: Shem, Ham, and Japheth. All the nations of the world can be traced back to these three men. Given that the world had been wiped out by the Flood, God could effectively eliminate two-thirds of the human race from the line of messiahship by specifying that the Messiah would come through the lineage of Shem, one of Noah's three sons.

Then continuing on down to the year 2000 BC, we find that God called a man named Abraham out of Ur of the Chaldeans. With Abraham, God became still more specific, stating that the Messiah would be one of his descendants. All the families of the earth would be blessed through Abraham (see Genesis 12:1-3; 17:1-8; 22:15-18). Many of Abraham's descendants were eliminated when God selected Isaac, the second son, and not Ishmael to be the ancestor of the Messiah (see Genesis 17:19-21; 21:12).

Isaac had two sons, Jacob and Esau. God chose the line of Jacob (see Genesis 28:1-4; 35:10-12; Numbers 24:17). Jacob had twelve sons, out of whose descendants developed the twelve tribes of Israel. Then God singled out the tribe of Judah for messiahship and eliminated eleven-twelfths of the Israelite tribes. And of all the family lines within the tribe of Judah, he chose the line of Jesse (see Isaiah 11:1-5). We can see the address narrowing.

Jesse had eight sons, and in 2 Samuel 7:12-16 and Jeremiah 23:5 God eliminated seven-eighths of Jesse's family line by choosing Jesse's son David. So in terms of lineage, the Messiah must be born of the seed of a woman, the lineage of Shem, a descendant of Abraham, the line of Isaac, the line of Jacob, the tribe of Judah, the family of Jesse, and the house of David.

In Micah 5:2 God eliminated all the cities of the world and selected Bethlehem, with a population of less than one thousand people at the time this prophecy was made, as the Messiah's birthplace.

Then through a series of prophecies he even defined the time period that would set

What do you think?

Have you ever explored your ancestry? Did you discover any interesting information about your family? Do you know anything about Jesus' ancestry? What do you find most interesting about it?

this man apart. For example, Malachi 3:1 and four other Old Testament verses require the Messiah to come while the Temple of Jerusalem is still standing (see Psalm 118:26; Daniel 9:26; Zechariah 11:13; Haggai 2:7-9). This is of great significance when we realize that the Temple was destroyed in AD 70 and has not since been rebuilt.

Isaiah 7:14 adds that Christ will be born of a virgin. A natural birth of unnatural conception was a criterion beyond human planning and control. Several prophecies recorded in Isaiah and the Psalms describe the social climate and response that God's man will encounter: his own people, the Jews, will reject him, and the Gentiles will believe in him (see Psalms 22:7-8; 118:22; Isaiah 8:14; 49:6; 50:6; 52:13-15). He will have a forerunner, a voice in the wilderness, one preparing the way before the Lord, a John the Baptist (see Isaiah 40:3-5; Malachi 3:1).

Notice how one passage in the New Testament (Matthew 27:3-10) refers to certain Old Testament prophecies that narrow down Christ's address even further. Matthew describes the events brought about by the actions of Judas after he betrayed Jesus. Matthew points out that these events were predicted in passages from the Old Testament (see Psalm 41:9; Zechariah 11:12-13).[1] In these passages God indicates that the Messiah will (1) be betrayed, (2) by a friend, (3) for thirty pieces of silver, and that the money will be (4) cast on the floor of the Temple. Thus the address becomes even more specific.

A prophecy dating from 1012 BC also predicts that this man's hands and feet will be pierced in a description that matches crucifixion (see Psalm 22:6-18; Zechariah 12:10; Galatians 3:13). This description of the manner of his death was written eight hundred years before the Romans used crucifixion as a method of execution.

The precise lineage; the place, time, and manner of birth; people's reactions; the betrayal; the manner of death—these are merely a fraction of the hundreds of details that make up the "address" to identify God's Son, the Messiah, the Savior of the world.

The precise lineage; the place, time, and manner of birth; the manner of death— these are merely a fraction of the hundreds of details that make up the "address" to identify God's Son, the Savior of the world.

Objection #1: The Prophecies Were Coincidental

A critic could claim, "Why, you could find some of these prophecies fulfilled in Abraham Lincoln, Anwar Sadat, John F. Kennedy, Mother Teresa, or Billy Graham."

Yes, I suppose one could possibly find one or two prophecies coincidental to other people, but not all of them. In fact, for years, the Christian Victory Publishing Company of Denver offered a one-thousand-dollar reward to anyone who could find any person other than Jesus, either living or dead, who could fulfill only half of the messianic predictions outlined in the book *Messiah in Both Testaments* by Fred John Meldau. They didn't get any takers.

Could one person fulfill all of the Old Testament prophecies? In their book *Science Speaks*, Peter Stoner and Robert Newman did calculations to analyze that probability. Writing in the foreword to that book, H. Harold Hartzler of the American Scientific Affiliation says,

The manuscript for *Science Speaks* has been carefully reviewed by a committee of the American Scientific Affiliation members and by the Executive Council of the same group and has been found, in general, to be dependable and accurate in regard to the scientific material presented. The mathematical analysis included is based upon principles of probability which are thoroughly sound, and Professor Stoner has applied these principles in a proper and convincing way.[2]

The following probabilities show that coincidence is ruled out. Stoner says that by applying the science of probability to eight prophecies, "we find that the chance that any man might have lived down to the present time and fulfilled all eight prophecies is 1 in 10^{17}"—that is, one in 100,000,000,000,000,000. To help us comprehend this staggering probability, Stoner illustrates it by supposing that

we take 10^{17} silver dollars and lay them on the face of Texas. They will cover all of the state two feet deep. Now mark one of these silver dollars and stir the whole mass thoroughly, all over the state. Blindfold a man and tell him that he can travel as far as he wishes, but he must pick up one silver dollar, and say that this is the right one. What chance would he have of getting the right one? Just the same chance that the prophets would have had of writing these eight prophecies and having them all come true in any one man, from their day to the present time, providing they wrote them in their own wisdom.

Now these prophecies were either given by inspiration of God or the prophets just wrote them as they thought they should be. In such a case the prophets had just one chance in 10^{17} of having them come true in any man, but they all came true in Christ.

What do you think?

How likely do you think it is for one person to literally fulfill so many ancient predictions that were said hundreds of years before the person was born? How is it possible that Jesus did?

Stoner continues, "This means that the fulfillment of these eight prophecies alone proves that God inspired the writing of those prophecies to a definiteness which lacks only one chance of 10^{17} of being absolute."[3]

Objection #2: The Prophecies Were Invented

Perhaps the most common objection is that the Gospel authors deliberately crafted their biographies of Jesus to make it appear that he fulfilled Old Testament prophecies. One obvious problem with this objection is the evidence that Jesus really did fulfill them! For instance, it is undeniable that Jesus uniquely brought representatives of all nations to a recognition of the God of Israel, fulfilling Isaiah 49:6. And there is compelling evidence for the destruction of the Temple within a generation of the life and ministry of Jesus, fulfilling Daniel 9:26.

Additionally, if the disciples invented the stories of fulfilled prophecy, then they were liars. But why invent a story to get themselves persecuted? The Jews were expecting a coming king, which gave them hope for release from Roman occupation. If the disciples' goal was to persuade people who longed for a conquering hero, they would have likely omitted or downplayed the crucifixion to craft a more convincing narrative. Invented prophecies aren't the most likely explanation.

Objection #3: Jesus Deliberately Fulfilled Them

Some claim that Jesus deliberately attempted to fulfill the Jewish prophecies. This objection seems plausible until we realize that many details of the Messiah's coming were totally beyond human control. One example is the place of his birth in Bethlehem, which is well supported by the evidence. When Herod asked the chief priests and scribes where the Christ was to be born, they replied, "In Bethlehem . . . for this is what the prophet wrote" (Matthew 2:5). It would be foolish to think that as Mary and Joseph traveled to the predicted town, Jesus, in his mother's womb, said, "Mom, you'd better hurry, or we won't make it."

Jesus also couldn't control his betrayal by Judas or the betrayal price; the manner of his death; the people's reaction, the mocking and spitting, the staring; the casting of dice for his clothes and the soldiers' hesitance to tear his garment. Furthermore, Christ couldn't cause himself to be born of the seed of a woman, in the lineage of Shem, descending from Abraham, and all of the other events that led to his birth. It's no wonder Jesus and the apostles appealed to fulfilled prophecy to substantiate his claim that he was the Son of God.

Why did God go to all this trouble? I believe he wanted Jesus Christ to have all the credentials he needed when he came into the world. Yet one of the most exciting things about Jesus is that he came to change lives. He alone fulfilled the Old Testament prophecies that anticipated his coming. And he alone can fulfill the greatest prophecy of all for those who will accept it—the promise of new life: "I will give you a new heart, and I will put a new spirit in you" (Ezekiel 36:26). "Anyone who belongs to Christ has become a new person. The old life is gone; a new life has begun!" (2 Corinthians 5:17).

> **Why did God go to all this trouble? I believe he wanted Jesus Christ to have all the credentials he needed when he came into the world. Yet one of the most exciting things about Jesus is that he came to change lives.**

CHAPTER 11

Isn't There Some Other Way?

During a lecture series at the University of Texas, a graduate student approached me and asked, "Why is Jesus the only way to a relationship with God?" I had shown that Jesus claimed to be the only way to God, that the testimony of the Scriptures and the apostles was reliable, and that there was sufficient evidence to warrant faith in Jesus as Savior and Lord. Yet the student still had questions: "Why Jesus only? Isn't there some other way to God?" Like this young man, people continually look for alternatives. "What about Buddha? Muhammad? Can't a person simply live a good life? If God is such a loving God, then won't he accept all people just the way they are?"

These questions are typical of what I often hear. In today's open climate, people seem offended by the exclusive claims that Jesus is the only way to God and the only source of forgiveness of sin and salvation. This attitude shows that many people simply don't understand the nature of God and the depth of their own sin. We can see the core of their misunderstanding in the question they usually ask: "How can a loving God allow anyone to go to hell?" I often turn the question around and ask, "How can a holy, just, and righteous God allow a sinful person into his presence?" Most people understand God to be a loving God, but they don't go any further. He is not only a God of love but also a God who is righteous, just, and holy. He cannot tolerate sin in his heaven any more than you would tolerate a filthy, foul-smelling, diseased dog to live in your home. This misunderstanding about the basic nature and character of God is the cause of many theological and ethical problems.

What do you think?

How would you describe God? Where did your ideas of God originate? Is there anything about Jesus that surprises you, that doesn't seem to fit your description of God?

Basically, we know God through his attributes. However, his attributes are not parts of him in the same way that the attributes you have adopted are parts of you. You may realize it is good to be courteous and adopt this attribute as a part of your overall makeup. With God it works the other way around. God's attributes, his very being, include such qualities as holiness, love, justice, and righteousness. For example, goodness is not a part of God but rather something that is true of God's very nature. God's attributes have their source in who God is. He didn't adopt them to make up his nature; they flow from his nature. So when we say God is love, we don't mean that a part of God is love but that love is an attribute that is innately true of God. When God loves, he is not deciding; he is simply being himself.

Here's the problem as it relates to us: If God's nature is love, how can he possibly send anyone to hell? The answer in a nutshell is that God doesn't send people to hell; they go because of their own choices. To explain, we must go all the way back to Creation. The Bible indicates that God created man and woman so he could share his love and glory with them. But Adam and Eve chose to rebel and go their own way. They left God's love and protection, contaminating themselves with that self-willed, grasping, prideful nature we call sin. Because God dearly loved the man and woman—even after they disobeyed him—he wanted to reach out to them and save them from the deadly path they had chosen. But God faced a dilemma. Because God is not only loving but also holy, righteous, and just, sin cannot survive in his presence. His very holy, just, and righteous nature would destroy the sinful couple. This is why the Bible says, "The wages of sin is death" (Romans 6:23). So how could God resolve this dilemma and save the man and woman?

The Godhead—God the Father, God the Son, and God the Holy Spirit—made an astounding decision. Jesus, God the Son, would take upon **God's attributes have their source in who God is. He didn't adopt them to make up his nature; they flow from his nature.**

himself human flesh. He would become the God-man. We read of this in the first chapter of the Gospel of John, where it says that "the Word became flesh, and dwelt among us" (1:14, NASB). Also, Philippians 2:6-7 tells us that Christ humbled himself and took on human form.

Jesus was the God-man. He was both divine and human. Jesus was just as much man as if he had never been God and just as much God as if he had never been man. His humanity did not diminish his deity, and his deity did not overpower his humanity. By his own choice he lived a sinless life, wholly obeying the Father. The biblical declaration that "the wages of sin is death" did not indict him. Because he was not only finite man but also infinite God, he had the infinite capacity to take on himself the sins of the world. When Jesus was executed on the cross more than two thousand years ago, God accepted his death as a substitute for ours. The just and righteous nature of God was satisfied. Justice was done; a penalty was paid. So at that point God's love and justice were perfectly satisfied, and he could accept us again and offer us what we had lost in Eden—that original relationship in which we could experience his love and glory.

Jesus was just as much man as if he had never been God and just as much God as if he had never been man.

Often I ask people, "For whom did Jesus die?" Usually they reply, "For me" or "For the world." And I will say, "Yes, that is right, but for whom else did Jesus die?" They generally admit that they don't know. I will reply, "For God the Father." You see, not only did Christ die for us, but he also died for the Father. This is addressed in the last section of Romans 3, where some versions of the Bible call the death of Jesus a "propitiation" (see verse 25, NASB). *Propitiation* basically means the satisfaction of a requirement. When Jesus died on the cross, he died not only for us but also to meet the holy and just requirements intrinsic to the basic nature of God. The contamination was removed so we could stand clean in his presence.

Several years ago I heard a true story that illuminates what Jesus did on the cross to solve God's problem in dealing with our sin. A young woman was stopped for speeding. The police officer ticketed her and took her before the judge. The judge read off the citation and asked, "Guilty or not guilty?" The woman replied, "Guilty." The judge brought down the gavel and fined her one hundred dollars or ten days in jail. Then he did an amazing thing. He stood up, took off his robe, stepped down from the bench, took out his billfold, and paid the young woman's fine. Why? The judge was her father. He loved his daughter, yet he was a just judge. She had broken the law, and he couldn't simply say to her, "Because I love you so much, I forgive you. You may go scot-free." Had he done such a thing, he would not have been a righteous judge. He would not have upheld the law. But because of his love for his daughter, he was willing to take off his judicial robe, step down to her position, assume his relationship as her father, and pay the fine.

This story illustrates in a small way what God did for us through Jesus Christ. We sinned, and the Bible says that "the wages of sin is death." When God looks at us, in

> **What do you think?**
> *Has anyone ever taken a punishment for you? Did your relationship with that person change after that? Would you be willing to do the same for that person, even if they deserved to be punished?*

> **What do you think?**
> *Do you find it difficult to forgive someone who has wronged you? What price do most people pay when they forgive others?*

spite of his tremendous love for us, he has to bring down the gavel and say *death* because he is a righteous and just God. And yet, because he is also a loving God, he was willing to come down off his throne in the form of the man Jesus Christ and pay the price for us, which was his death on the cross.

At this point many people ask the natural question, "Why couldn't God just forgive without requiring any payment?" An executive in a large corporation once told me, "My employees often damage equipment, waste materials, and break things, and I just forgive them. Are you telling me I can do something God can't do?" The executive failed to realize that his forgiveness cost him something. His company paid for his employees' failures by repairing and replacing damaged items. Wherever there is forgiveness, there is payment. For example, let's say my daughter breaks a lamp in my home. I'm a loving and forgiving father, so I hug her and say, "Don't cry, honey. Daddy loves you and forgives you." Usually the person who hears that story will say, "That's exactly what God ought to do." Then comes the question, "Who pays for the lamp?" The fact is, *I* do. Forgiveness always has a price. Let's say someone insults you in front of others, and later you graciously say, "I forgive you." Who bears the price of that insult? You do. You bear the pain of what was said and the loss of reputation in the eyes of those who witnessed the insult.

Forgiveness always has a price. God has paid the price for our forgiveness himself through the Cross. It's a payment that any other religious or ethical leader cannot offer.

This is what God has done for us: he has said, "I forgive

you." But he paid the price for the forgiveness himself through the Cross. It's a payment that Buddha, Muhammad, Confucius, or any other religious or ethical leader cannot offer. No one can pay the price by "just living a good life." I know it sounds exclusive to say it, but we must say it simply because it is true: there is no other way but Jesus.

CHAPTER 12

He Changed My Life

What I have shared with you in this book is what I learned after digging through the evidence for Christianity after my friends at the university challenged me to prove the truth of their claims. You would think that after examining the evidence, I would have immediately jumped on board and become a Christian. But in spite of the abundant evidence, I felt a strong reluctance to take the plunge. My mind was convinced of the truth. I had to admit that Jesus Christ must be exactly who he claimed to be. I could plainly see that Christianity was not a myth, not a fantasy of wishful dreamers, not a hoax played on the simpleminded, but rock-solid truth. I knew the truth, yet my will was pulling me in another direction.

There were two reasons for my reluctance: pleasure and pride. I thought that becoming a Christian meant giving up the good life and giving up control. I could sense Jesus Christ at the door of my heart, pleading, "Look, I have been standing at your door and constantly knocking. If you hear me calling and will open the door, I will come in" (see Revelation 3:20). I kept that door shut and bolted. I didn't care if he did walk on water or turn water into wine. I didn't want any party pooper spoiling my fun. I couldn't think of any faster way to ruin my good times. The truth is, I called them good times, but I was really miserable. I was a walking battlefield. My mind was telling me that Christianity was true, but my will was resisting it with all the energy it could muster.

My mind was telling me that Christianity was true, but my will was resisting it with all the energy it could muster.

Then there was the pride problem. At that time the thought of becoming a Christian shattered my ego. I had just proved that all my previous thinking had been wrong and my friends had been right. Every time I got around those enthusiastic Christians, the inner conflict would boil over. If you've ever been in the company of happy people when you are miserable, you know how their joy can get under your skin. Sometimes I would literally get up, leave the group, and run right out of the student union. It came to the point where I would go to bed at ten o'clock at night but wouldn't get to sleep until four in the morning. I couldn't let go of the problem. I had to do something before it drove me out of my mind.

I always tried to be open-minded, but not so open-minded that my brains would fall out. As G. K. Chesterton says, "The object of opening the mind, as of opening the mouth, is to shut it again on something solid."[1] I opened my mind, and I finally closed it on the most solid reality I had ever experienced. On December 19, 1959, at 8:30 p.m., during my second year at the university, I became a Christian. The evidence had gotten my attention, but it was the love of God that drew me. As the apostle Paul noted, it is God's kindness that leads to repentance (see Romans 2:4).

Someone asked me, "How do you know you became a Christian?" One of several answers was simple: "It has changed my life." It is this transformation that assures me of the validity of my conversion. That night I prayed

> **What do you think?**
> Now that you are at the end of the book, have any of your thoughts about Jesus Christ changed? Are you challenged to read more about him? To talk to others who have given their lives to him?

four things to establish a relationship with the resurrected, living Christ, and I am grateful that this prayer has been answered.

First, I said, "Lord Jesus, thank you for dying on the cross for me." Second, I said, "I confess those things in my life that aren't pleasing to you and ask you to forgive and cleanse me." God tells us, "No matter how deep the stain of your sins, I can remove it. I can make you as clean as freshly fallen snow" (see Isaiah 1:18). Third, I said, "Right now, in the best way I know how, I open the door of my heart and life and trust you as my Savior and Lord. Take control of my life. Change me from the inside out. Make me the type of person you created me to be." The last thing I prayed was "Thank you for coming into my life by faith." It was a faith based not on ignorance but on evidence, the facts of history, and God's Word.

I'm sure you have heard people speak of the "bolt of lightning" that hit them when they had their first religious experience. Well, it wasn't that dramatic for me. After I prayed, nothing happened. I mean *nothing*. And I still haven't sprouted wings or a halo. In fact, after I made that decision, I felt worse. I actually felt that I was about to vomit. *Oh no, what have I gotten sucked into now?* I wondered. I really felt I had gone off the deep end (and I'm sure some people thought I did!).

In six to eighteen months, I knew I had not gone off the deep end. My life *was* changed. The change was not immediate, but it was real. At about that time I was in a debate with the head of the history department at a Midwestern university. I was telling him about my new life, and he interrupted me with, "McDowell, are you trying to tell me that God has really changed your life? Give me some specifics." After listening to me explain for forty-five minutes, he finally said, "Okay, okay, that's enough!"

My faith is based not on ignorance but on evidence, the facts of history, and God's Word.

One change I told him about was relief from my restlessness. Before I accepted Christ, I always had to be occupied. I had to be over at my girlfriend's place, at a party, at the student union, or running around with friends. I'd walk across the campus with my mind in a whirlwind of conflicts. I was always bouncing off the walls. I'd sit down and try to study or reflect but couldn't do it. After I made that decision for Christ, a kind of mental peace settled over me. Don't misunderstand; I don't mean all conflicts ceased. What I found in this relationship with Jesus wasn't

so much the absence of conflict as the ability to cope with
it. I wouldn't trade that for
anything in the world.

What do you think?
If there was one area of
your life that you would
like God to change,
what would it be?

Another area that began to
change was my bad temper. I
used to blow my stack if any-
one just looked at me cross-eyed. I still have the scars from
a fight in which I almost killed a man my first year in the
university. My temper was such a part of me that I didn't
consciously seek to change it. But one day I encountered a
crisis that should have set me off, only to find that I stayed
calm and collected. My temper was gone! It wasn't my
doing; as I've been telling you, Jesus changed my life. That
doesn't mean I was perfect. I went fourteen years without
losing my temper, but when I did blow it, I'm afraid I made
up for all those times I didn't.

Jesus changed me in another way. I'm not proud of
it, but I mention it because many people need the same
change, and I want to show them the source of that change:
a relationship with the resurrected, living Christ. The problem is hatred. I had a heavy load of hatred weighing me
down. It didn't show outwardly, but it kept grinding away
inwardly. I was ticked off with people, with things, with
issues. I was insecure. Every time I met anyone different
from me, that person became
a threat, and I reacted with
some level of hatred.

I hated one man more than
anyone else in the world—my
father. I hated his guts. I was
mortified because he was the

**What I found in this
relationship with
Jesus wasn't so
much the absence of
conflict as the ability
to cope with it.**

town alcoholic. If you're from a small town and one of your parents is an alcoholic, you know what I mean. Everybody knows. My high school friends would make jokes about my father's drinking. They didn't think it bothered me because I fell in with the joking and laughed with them. I was laughing on the outside, but let me tell you, I was crying on the inside. I would go to the barn and find my mother beaten so badly she couldn't get up, lying in the manure behind the cows. When we had friends over, because he was drunk, I would take my father out to the barn, tie him up, and park his car behind the silo. We would tell our guests he'd had to go somewhere. I don't think anyone could hate a person more than I hated my father.

About five months after I made that decision for Christ, a love from God entered my life so powerfully that it took that hatred, turned it upside down, and emptied it out.

I hated one man more than anyone else in the world—my father. After I made that decision for Christ, a love from God entered my life so powerfully that it took that hatred, turned it upside down, and emptied it out.

I was able to look my father squarely in the eyes and say, "Dad, I love you." And I really meant it. After some of the things I'd done to him, that really shook him up.

After I transferred to a private university, a serious car accident put me in the hospital. When I was moved home to recover, my father came to visit me. Remarkably, he was sober that day. But he seemed uneasy, pacing about the room. Then he blurted out, "Son, how can you love a father like me?" I answered, "Dad, six months ago I despised you." Then I shared with him the story of my research and conclusions about Jesus Christ. I told him, "I have placed my trust in Christ, received God's forgiveness, invited him into my life, and he has changed me. I can't explain it all, Dad, but God has taken away my hatred and replaced it with the capacity to love. I love you and accept you just the way you are."

We talked for almost an hour, and then I received one of the greatest thrills of my life. This man who was my father, this man who knew me too well for me to pull the wool over his eyes, looked at me and said, "Son, if God can do in my life what I've seen him do in yours, then I want to give him the opportunity. I want to trust him as my Savior and Lord." I cannot imagine a greater miracle.

What do you think?

Why is it difficult to separate the faith of Christianity from the person of Jesus Christ? Can you see how the two are often viewed as being in opposition?

Usually after a person accepts Christ, the changes in his or her life occur over a period of days, weeks, months, or even years. In my own life the change took about six to eighteen months. But the life of my father was transformed right before my eyes. It was as if God reached down and flipped on the light switch. Never before or since have I seen such a dramatic change. My father touched an alcoholic beverage only once after that day. He got it as far as his lips before thrusting it away. Forever. I can come to only one conclusion: a relationship with Jesus Christ changes lives.

There was another person in my life that I needed to forgive. His name was Wayne, a man who worked for my parents when I was growing up on the farm. When my mom had to run an errand or was gone for a longer period of time, she put Wayne in charge of me. Mom would march me up to Wayne and say, "Now you obey Wayne and do everything he asks you to do. If you don't, you are going to get a thrashing when I get home." Trust me; you didn't want to get a thrashing from my mother.

But I would have gladly taken the thrashings if I had known what Wayne had in store for me. From the time I was six years old until I was thirteen, he sexually abused me regularly. When I told my mother, she refused to believe me. At thirteen, I threatened Wayne. "If you ever touch me again, I will kill you." Wayne knew I was serious, and he stopped.

I wanted Wayne to burn in hell, and I was willing to escort him there. The memories of the abuse scarred me. But after coming to Christ, I knew I needed to forgive Wayne, just as I had forgiven my father. I confronted Wayne once again and said, "Wayne, what you did to me was evil. But I've trusted Jesus Christ as Savior and Lord and have become a Christian. I've come to tell you that Jesus died as much for you as he did for me. I forgive you." It was one of the most difficult things I've ever had to do. I could never have done it on my own. If you have a similar story, be assured that you don't have to face your demons alone either. Your past *can* be overcome with God's help and with the help of others.

You can laugh at Christianity; you can mock it and ridicule it. But it's true and it works. It changes lives. I should say *Jesus Christ* changes lives. Christianity is not merely a religion; it's not a system; it's not an ethical ideal; it's not a psychological phenomenon. It is focused on the person and work of Jesus Christ. If you trust Christ, start watching your attitudes and actions, because Jesus Christ is in the business of changing lives. He changed mine, and he can change yours.

So as you can see, finding my faith in Christ has been a process, beginning with hard-nosed research and growing into the experience of a changed life. It seems that many people today are eager for the experience—they want the kind of renewed life that I've found—but they are unwilling to put Christianity to the hard rational and evidential test. Maybe part of their reluctance is a hesitance to affirm that anything is absolutely true in the face of today's emphasis on pluralism and inclusion. Or maybe it stems from a fear that their exploration would raise doubts rather than affirm the truth of Christ's claims.

Christianity is not merely a religion; it's not a system; it's not an ethical ideal; it's not a psychological phenomenon. It is focused on the person of Jesus Christ, who is in the business of changing lives.

Is research a hindrance to one's faith in Christ? Not according to Edwin Yamauchi, a Japanese American historian who is one of the world's leading experts in ancient history. Yamauchi, who was raised as a Buddhist, is emphatic: "For me, the historical evidence has reinforced my commitment to Jesus Christ as the Son of God who loves us and died for us and was raised from the dead. It's that simple."[2]

When asked if historical New Testament scholarship had weakened his faith, ancient manuscript authority Bruce Metzger immediately replied, "It has built it. I've asked questions all my life. I've dug into the text, I've studied this thoroughly, and today I know with confidence that my trust in Jesus has been well placed . . . very well placed."[3]

Quotations such as these from two respected scholars affirm my purpose in writing this little book. I have tried to show you that the claims of Christ stand firm as solid historical facts, confirmed by the evidence of history, prophecy, and reason. Understanding the facts will give you a solid, dependable foundation to stand on as you experience Christ's claims for yourself in the kind of changed lives that I and millions of other Christians have experienced.

But in spite of the firmness of the facts and the authenticity of the experience, Christianity is not something you can shove down anyone's throat. You can't force Christ on anyone. You've got to live your life, and I've got to live mine. All of us are free to make our own decisions. All I can do is tell you what I've learned. After that, what you do is up to you.

Perhaps the prayer I prayed will help you: "Lord Jesus, I need you. Thank you for dying on the cross for me. Forgive me and cleanse me. At this very moment I trust you as Savior and Lord. Make me the type of person you created me to be. In Christ's name, Amen."

Praise for *More Than a Carpenter*

As I read *More Than a Carpenter*, I realized how little I knew about Christianity. I had already made so many judgments about the Bible and Jesus without really knowing any facts. I learned that there was so much evidence for Jesus. As I read the book, I knew that it was time to know God in my heart!

   Reader from Estonia

More than a Carpenter . . . saved my dad's life. He stopped drinking and gave his heart to the Lord. Once all his kids saw the change in him, the peace and joy, we all wanted it, and eventually all of us gave our hearts to the Lord.

   Reader from the United States

Your book cleared up doubts that I knew I had and some I didn't even know existed inside of me.

   Reader from Maryland Division of Corrections

I was looking in a shop for greeting cards. As I left the store, a man handed me *More Than a Carpenter* as a gift. That evening I could not put it down. I found the content very interesting, and I did not sleep until I had finished reading it. The next day I shared the book with friends, and we all passed it around and read it and then discussed it together. Then as a small group we decided this is the truth.

   Reader from the Middle East

More Than a Carpenter has become my favorite book. I have bought many and given them away.

Reader from the United States

Notes

CHAPTER 1: MY STORY

1. Aquinas wrote, "The will tends naturally to its last end; for every man naturally wills happiness: and all other desires are caused by this natural desire; since whatever a man wills he wills on account of the end" (Aquinas, *Summa Theologica* 1a 60.2c).

CHAPTER 2: WHAT MAKES JESUS SO DIFFERENT?

1. Archibald Thomas Robertson, *Word Pictures in the New Testament* (Nashville: Broadman Press, 1932), 5:187.

2. Charles F. Pfeiffer and Everett F. Harrison, eds., *The Wycliffe Bible Commentary* (Chicago: Moody, 1962), 943–944 (on the parallel passage in Matthew 9:5).

3. Lewis Sperry Chafer, *Systematic Theology* (Dallas: Dallas Seminary Press, 1948), 5:21.

4. Robert M. Bowman Jr. and J. Ed Komoszewski, *Putting Jesus in His Place: The Case for the Deity of Christ* (Grand Rapids: Kregel, 2007), 246–247.

5. Robert Anderson, *The Lord from Heaven* (Grand Rapids: Kregel, 1978 [orig. 1910]), 22.

6. Henry Barclay Swete, *The Gospel According to St. Mark*, 3rd ed. (London: Macmillan, 1920), 360.

7. Irwin H. Linton, *The Sanhedrin Verdict* (New York: Loizeaux Bros., 1943), 7.

8. William Jay Gaynor, "The Trial of Jesus from a Legal Standpoint," in Alvin V. Sellers, *Classics of the Bar*, vol. 2 (Baxley, GA: Classic Publishing, 1911), 30.

CHAPTER 3: LORD, LIAR, OR LUNATIC?

1. C. S. Lewis, *Mere Christianity* (New York: Macmillan, 1960), 40–41.

2. F. J. A. Hort, *Way, Truth, and the Life* (New York: Macmillan, 1894), 207.

3. Kenneth Scott Latourette, *A History of Christianity* (New York: Harper & Row, 1953), 44, 48.

4. William E. Lecky, *History of European Morals from Augustus to Charlemagne* (New York: D. Appleton, 1903), 2:8–9.

5. Philip Schaff, *History of the Christian Church* (Grand Rapids: Eerdmans, 1962), 109.

6. Philip Schaff, *The Person of Christ* (New York: American Tract Society, 1913), 94–95.

7. Personal email correspondence with Sean McDowell on September 11, 2023.

8. Pablo Martinez and Andrew Sims, *Mad or God? Jesus: The Healthiest Mind of All* (Downers Grove, IL: InterVarsity, 2018), 93.

9. Gary R. Collins, quoted in Lee Strobel, *The Case for Christ* (Grand Rapids: Zondervan, 1998), 147.

10. C. S. Lewis, *Miracles: A Preliminary Study* (New York: Macmillan, 1947), 113.

11. Schaff, *Person of Christ*, 97.

CHAPTER 4: WHAT ABOUT SCIENCE?

1. *The New Encyclopedia Brittanica: Micropaedia*, 15th ed. (2009), s.v. "scientific method."

2. James B. Conant, *Science and Common Sense* (New Haven, CT: Yale University Press, 1951), 25.

CHAPTER 5: IS THE NEW TESTAMENT RELIABLE?

1. John A. T. Robinson, *Redating the New Testament* (London: SCM Press, 1976).

2. Jonathan Bernier, *Rethinking the Dates of the New Testament: The Evidence for Early Composition* (Grand Rapids: Baker Academic, 2022), 1.

3. Sir William Ramsay, *The Bearing of Recent Discovery on the Trustworthiness of the New Testament* (London: Hodder and Stoughton, 1915), 222.

4. Craig S. Keener, *Acts: An Exegetical Commentary: Introduction and 1:1–2:47*, vol. 1 (Grand Rapids: Baker Academic, 2012), 217.

5. Simon Kistemaker, *The Gospels in Current Study* (Grand Rapids: Baker, 1972), 48–49.

6. A. H. McNeile, *An Introduction to the Study of the New Testament*, rev. by C. S. C. Williams, 2nd ed. (London: Oxford University Press, 1953), 54.

7. Paul L. Maier, *First Easter: The True and Unfamiliar Story in Words and Pictures* (New York: Harper & Row, 1973), 122.

8. Philip Jenkins, *Hidden Gospels: How the Search for Jesus Lost Its Way* (New York: Oxford University Press, 2001), 83.

9. Quoted in Jenkins, 98–99.

10. Chauncey Sanders, *Introduction to Research in English Literary History* (New York: Macmillan, 1952), 143ff.

11. Katie Leggett and Greg Paulson, "How Many Greek New Testament Manuscripts Are There REALLY? The Latest Numbers," *Institute for New Testament Textual Research* (blog), September 29, 2023, https://ntvmr.uni-muenster.de/en_US/intfblog/-/blogs/how-many-greek-new-testament-manuscripts-are-there-really-the-latest-numbers.

12. According to Graeme D. Bird, a specialist of *Iliad* manuscripts, "Homer's *Iliad* is currently represented by more than 1,900 manuscripts (at least 1,500 of which are on papyrus, although many of these of a fragmentary nature)." "Textual Criticism as Applied to Classical and Biblical Texts," in *Multitextuality in the Homeric Iliad: The Witness of the Ptolemaic Papyri*, (Washington, DC: Center for Hellenic Studies, 2010).

13. Daniel B. Wallace, ed., *Revisiting the Corruption of the New Testament: Manuscript, Patristic, and Apocryphal Evidence*, Text and Canon of the New Testament (Grand Rapids: Kregel, 2011), 28–29.

14. For more information on the value of later manuscripts, see Gregory R. Lanier's contribution in chapter 6 of *Myths and Mistakes in New Testament Textual Criticism*, ed. Elijah Hixson and Peter J. Gurry (Downers Grove, IL: IVP Academic, 2019).

15. Giorgio Pasquali, *Storia della tradizione e critica del testo*, 2nd ed. (Florence: Le Monnier, 1952), 8.

16. Hixson and Gurry, *Myths and Mistakes*, 194.

17. Michael Bruce Morrill, "A Complete Collation and Analysis of All Greek Manuscripts of John 18" (PhD thesis, University of Birmingham, 2012).

18. Hixson and Gurry, *Myths and Mistakes*, 196.

19. J. Ed Komoszewski, M. James Sawyer, and Daniel B. Wallace, *Reinventing Jesus: How Contemporary Skeptics Miss the Real Jesus and Mislead Popular Culture* (Grand Rapids: Kregel, 2006), 109.

20. John Warwick Montgomery, *Where Is History Going?* (Grand Rapids: Zondervan, 1969), 46.

21. Louis R. Gottschalk, *Understanding History* (New York: Knopf, 1969), 150.

22. J. Warner Wallace, *Cold-Case Christianity: A Homicide Detective Investigates the Claims of the Gospels* (Colorado Springs: David C. Cook, 2023), 198.

23. F. F. Bruce, *The New Testament Documents: Are They Reliable?* (Downer's Grove, IL: InterVarsity, 1964), 33.

24. David Hackett Fischer, *Historians' Fallacies: Toward a Logic of Historical Thought*, quoted in Norman L. Geisler, *Why I Am a Christian* (Grand Rapids: Baker, 2001), 152.

25. Will Durant, *Caesar and Christ: The Story of Civilization: Part III* (New York: Simon and Schuster, 1944), 557.

26. Gary R. Habermas, *On the Resurrection*, vol. 1, *Evidences* (Brentwood, TN: B & H Academic, 2024), 212–218.

27. Titus Kennedy, *Unearthing the Bible: 101 Archaeological Discoveries That Bring the Bible to Life* (Eugene, OR: Harvest House, 2020), 9–10.

28. F. F. Bruce, "Archaeological Confirmation of the New Testament," *Revelation and the Bible*, ed. Carl Henry (Grand Rapids: Baker, 1969), 331.

29. Lydia McGrew, *Testimonies to the Truth: Why You Can Trust the Gospels* (Tampa, FL: DeWard Publishing, 2023).

CHAPTER 6: WHO WOULD DIE FOR A LIE?

1. Richard Bauckham, *Jesus and the Eyewitnesses: The Gospels as Eyewitness Testimony*, 2nd ed. (Grand Rapids: Eerdmans, 2017), 116.

2. Lydia McGrew, *Testimonies to the Truth: Why You Can Trust the Gospels* (Tampa, FL: DeWard Publishing, 2023), 9–10.

3. McGrew, 10.

4. Flavius Josephus, *Antiquities of the Jews*, xx, 9:1.

5. J. P. Moreland, quoted in Lee Strobel, *The Case for Christ* (Grand Rapids: Zondervan, 1998), 248.

6. Edward Gibbon, quoted in Philip Schaff, *History of the Christian Church* (Peabody, MA: Hendrickson, 1996), chap. 3.

7. Michael Green, "Editor's Preface" in George Eldon Ladd, *I Believe in the Resurrection of Jesus* (Grand Rapids: Eerdmans, 1975), vii.

8. Blaise Pascal, quoted in Robert W. Gleason, ed., *The Essential Pascal*, trans. G. F. Pullen (New York: Mentor-Omega Books, 1966), 187.

9. Sean McDowell, *The Fate of the Apostles: Examining the Martyrdom Accounts of the Closest Followers of Jesus* (London, UK: Routledge Press, 2018), 264–265.

10. Michael Green, *Man Alive!* (Downers Grove, IL: InterVarsity, 1968), 23–24.

11. Kenneth Scott Latourette, *A History of Christianity* (New York: Harper & Brothers Publishers, 1937), 1:59.

12. N.T. Wright, *Christian Origins and the Question of God*, vol. 3, *The Resurrection of the Son of God* (Minneapolis: Fortress Press, 2003), 10.

13. Simon Greenleaf, *An Examination of the Testimony of the Four Evangelists by the Rules of Evidence Administered in the Courts of Justice* (Grand Rapids: Baker, 1965), 29.

14. William Lane Craig, quoted in Strobel, *Case for Christ*, 220.

CHAPTER 7: WHAT GOOD IS A DEAD MESSIAH?

1. Encyclopedia International (New York: Grolier, 1972), 4:407.

2. Ernest Findlay Scott, *The Kingdom and the Messiah* (Edinburgh: T&T Clark, 1911), 55.

3. Joseph Klausner, *The Messianic Idea in Israel* (New York: Macmillan, 1955), 23.

4. Jacob Gartenhaus, "The Jewish Conception of the Messiah," *Christianity Today*, March 13, 1970, 8–10.

5. *Jewish Encyclopedia* (New York: Funk and Wagnalls, 1906), 8:508.

6. A. B. Bruce, *The Training of the Twelve* (Grand Rapids: Kregel, 1971), 177.

7. Alfred Edersheim, *Sketches of Jewish Social Life in the Days of Christ* (Grand Rapids: Eerdmans, 1960), 29.

8. Pinchas Lapide, *The Resurrection of Jesus: A Jewish Perspective* (London: SPCK, 1983), 125.

CHAPTER 8: DID YOU HEAR WHAT HAPPENED TO SAUL?

1. Jacques Dupont, "The Conversion of Paul, and Its Influence on His Understanding of Salvation by Faith," *Apostolic History and the Gospel*, ed. W. Ward Gasque and Ralph P. Martin (Grand Rapids: Eerdmans, 1970), 177.

2. Michael R. Licona, *The Resurrection of Jesus: A New Historiographical Approach* (Downers Grove, IL: InterVarsity, 2010), 440.

3. Douglas A. Campbell, *Paul: An Apostle's Journey* (Grand Rapids: Eerdmans, 2018), 22.

4. Dupont, "Conversion of Paul," 76.

5. Philip Schaff, *History of the Christian Church* (Grand Rapids: Eerdmans, 1910), 1:296.

6. *Encyclopaedia Britannica*, vol. 17 (United States: The Encyclopedia Britannica, Inc., 1970), s.v. "Paul, Saint."

7. Archibald McBride, quoted in *Chambers's Encyclopedia* (London: Pergamon Press, 1966), 10:516.

8. George Lyttelton, *The Conversion of St. Paul* (New York: American Tract Society, 1929), 467.

CHAPTER 9: CAN YOU KEEP A GOOD MAN DOWN?

1. Alexander Metherell, quoted in Lee Strobel, *The Case for Christ* (Grand Rapids: Zondervan, 1998), 195–196.

2. John Dominic Crossan, *Jesus: A Revolutionary Biography* (New York: HarperOne, 1995), 145.

3. George Currie, *The Military Discipline of the Romans from the Founding of the City to the Close of the Republic*. An abstract of a thesis published under the auspices of the Graduate Council of Indiana University, 1928, 41–43.

4. A. T. Robertson, *Word Pictures in the New Testament* (New York: R. R. Smith, 1931), 239.

5. Arthur Michael Ramsey, *God, Christ and the World* (London: SCM Press, 1969), 78–80.

6. James Hastings, ed., *Dictionary of the Apostolic Church* (New York: C. Scribner's Sons, 1916), 2:340.

7. Paul Althaus, quoted in Wolfhart Pannenberg, *Jesus—God and Man*, trans. Lewis L. Wilkins and Duane A. Priebe (Philadelphia: Westminster Press, 1968), 100.

8. Paul L. Maier, "The Empty Tomb as History," *Christianity Today*, March 28, 1975, 5.

9. Craig S. Keener, *A Commentary on the Gospel of Matthew* (Grand Rapids: Eerdmans, 1999), 713–714.

10. Keener, 714, footnotes 333, 334.

11. David Friedrich Strauss, *The Life of Jesus for the People* (London: Williams and Norgate, 1879), 1: 412.

12. J. N. D. Anderson, *Christianity: The Witness of History* (London: Tyndale Press, 1969), 92.

13. John Warwick Montgomery, *History and Christianity* (Downers Grove, IL: InterVarsity, 1972), 78.

14. Jodi Magness, "Has the Tomb of Jesus Been Discovered?" *Biblical Archaeology Society*, March 5, 2007, https://www.biblicalarchaeology.org/daily/archaeology-today/biblical-archaeology-topics/has-the-tomb-of-jesus-been-discovered/.

15. Craig Evans and Steven Feldman, "The Tomb of Jesus? Wrong on Every Count," *Biblical Archaeology Society*, February 1, 2023, https://www.biblicalarchaeology.org/daily/archaeology-today/biblical-archaeology-topics/the-tomb-of-jesus-wrong-on-every-count/.

16. Magness, "Has the Tomb of Jesus Been Discovered?"

17. Paul Rhodes Eddy and Gregory A. Boyd, *The Jesus Legend: A Case for the Historical Reliability of the Synoptic Jesus Tradition* (Grand Rapids: Baker Books, 2007), 142.

18. T. N. D. Mettinger, *The Riddle of Resurrection: "Dying and Rising Gods" in the Ancient Near East* (Stockholm: Almqvist and Wiksell, 2001), 221.

19. Thomas Arnold, *Christian Life—Its Hopes, Its Fears, and Its Close* (London: T. Fellowes, 1859), 324.

20. Brooke Foss Westcott, quoted in Paul E. Little, *Know Why You Believe* (Wheaton, IL: Scripture Press, 1967), 70.

21. William Lane Craig, *Assessing the New Testament Evidence for the Historicity of the Resurrection of Jesus* (Lewiston, NY: The Edwin Mellen Press, 1989), 418.

22. Simon Greenleaf, *An Examination of the Testimony of the Four Evangelists by the Rules of Evidence Administered in the Courts of Justice* (Grand Rapids: Baker, 1965), 29.

23. Ross Clifford, *Leading Lawyers' Case for the Resurrection* (Edmonton, Canada: Canadian Institute for Law, Theology, & Public Policy, 1991), 112.

24. Clifford, 112.

25. Frank Morison, *Who Moved the Stone?* (London: Faber and Faber, 1930).

26. Lord Darling, quoted in Michael Green, *Man Alive!* (Downers Grove, IL: InterVarsity, 1968), 54.

CHAPTER 10: WILL THE REAL MESSIAH PLEASE STAND UP?

1. Matthew attributes the passage he quotes in 27:9-10 to the prophet Jeremiah, but the passage actually occurs in Zechariah 11:12-13. The apparent discrepancy is resolved when we understand the organization of the Hebrew canon. Hebrew Scriptures were divided into three sections: law, writings, and prophets. Jeremiah came first in their order of prophetic books, and thus Hebrew scholars often found it an acceptable shortcut to refer to the entire collection of prophetic writings by the name of the first book—Jeremiah.

2. H. Harold Hartzler, from the foreword to Peter W. Stoner, *Science Speaks* (Chicago: Moody, 1963).

3. Stoner, 107.

CHAPTER 12: HE CHANGED MY LIFE

1. G. K. Chesterton, *The Autobiography of G. K. Chesterton* (San Francisco: Ignatius, 2006), 217.
2. Edwin Yamauchi, quoted in Lee Strobel, *The Case for Christ* (Grand Rapids: Zondervan, 1998), 90.
3. Strobel, 71.

About the Authors

For over sixty years **Josh McDowell** has provided break through moments for more than forty-six million people in 139 countries about the evidence for Christianity and the transformative difference it makes. Through his work with Cru and the global reach of Josh McDowell Ministry, millions of people worldwide have encountered the love of Christ.

He is the author or coauthor of more than 160 books, including *Evidence That Demands a Verdict*, *12 Crucial Truths of the Christian Faith*, *Why Did God Do That?*, and *How to Know God Exists*. Josh and his wife, Dottie, live in Dana Point, California, and have four grown children and eleven grandchildren.

Sean McDowell is a professor of Christian Apologetics at Talbot School of Theology, Biola University. He is the author, coauthor, or editor of over twenty books, including *A Rebel's Manifesto*, *Set Adrift*, *Is God Just a Human Invention?*, *Apologetics Study Bible for Students*, and *End the Stalemate*.

Sean has taught high school full-time or part-time for over two decades and was named Educator of the Year for San Juan Capistrano in 2008. He hosts one of the leading apologetics channels on YouTube and is the cohost of the *Think Biblically* podcast. He is an internationally recognized speaker. You can follow Sean on social media and contact him for speaking events at seanmcdowell.org/.

In April 2000, Sean married his high school sweetheart, Stephanie. They have three children and live in San Juan Capistrano, California.

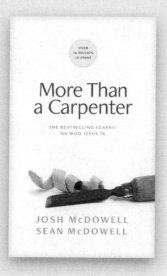

Sharing Truth With
A New Generation

SeanMcDowell.org

Sean_McDowell
Sean_McDowell
SeanMcDowell
Dr. Sean McDowell
Podcast: The Think Biblically Podcast